Quick Cooking

MARY BERRY

Quick Cooking

BOOKS

Contents

Introduction

We lead such busy lives these days that it's all too easy to become reliant on convenience foods. Finding time to cook a meal yourself can seem daunting – so much easier to pop something in the microwave or buy a takeaway. But making a dish from scratch doesn't have to be time-consuming and nothing beats good home cooking in terms of flavour or nutritional value. For this book, I've assembled a range of delicious, easy dishes that can be put together as quickly as possible using a mixture of fresh ingredients and store-cupboard staples.

You'll find weeknight dishes that can be on the table in under 30 minutes; recipes that can be made ahead of time and then cooked or assembled when you're ready; wonderful quick roasts and satisfying stews that can be on the table much faster than traditional options but without any loss of flavour; simple fresh salads and vegetable dishes; and easy-to-prepare meals that cook while you do something else.

Foolproof Quick Cooking

To achieve great flavour with no fuss, first and foremost you need quality ingredients. Try to buy the best that you can afford, as this will actually save you time. When something is fresh and in season, it will be full of flavour and will need only a few other ingredients to set it off, making it quicker to prepare. Think of tender asparagus or pink-stemmed rhubarb in early spring or locally grown strawberries and raspberries in the summer. Buy local if you can – if you know where your food comes from, it tastes even better! Fresh ingredients don't have to be costly – go to your local market or farm shop to hunt out bargains and buy whatever is in season. If a particular ingredient isn't available, you can easily swap it for another one, as I suggest in many of my recipes. And always check in your fridge, to see what you have already and might be able to use. This can help save you time as well as money. Leftover mashed potato can be made into potato cakes in a variety of flavours (see page 200), for example, while roast chicken can be sliced up for a nourishing bowl of Chicken Noodle Soup (see page 68).

Salads are perfect for putting together a range of complementary flavours, textures and colours and are so quick to make. You'll find a lovely selection to choose from here, from delicious crunchy slaws to more sustaining dishes using grains such as bulgur wheat or quinoa. On cooler days, soups always go down well and I've included a good selection here, from the easy, no-blend Everyday Vegetable Soup on page 58, for which you could use any root vegetables you have to hand, to the wonderfully warming Smoky Red Pepper and Bean Soup on page 63 – so simple to knock up with a tin of cannellini beans.

People are often wary about cooking fish, yet it's one of the quickest foods to prepare. One of the simplest ways is to oven-bake it in a foil parcel with a few flavourings – see my Sea Bass en Papillote with Courgette Ribbons on page 108. Scallops, a real treat for a special occasion, take next to no time to cook on the hob (see page 117). Or you could just take advantage of ready-cooked seafood, such as the prawns and crayfish tails in my version of the Indonesian classic, Nasi Goreng, on page 171.

Quick Techniques

When it comes to cooking, bear in mind that the size of the ingredients makes a difference to how long it will take. A smaller cut of meat will cook in a fraction of the time of a large joint, for example, but is just as tasty. Take the Marinated Rosemary Lamb Steaks with Red Peppers on page 160, or the roast loin of venison on page 143 – rolled in crushed peppercorns for extra flavour, this is roasted in the oven very briefly (only 12 minutes) and served with a creamy peppercorn sauce. Like venison, beef and lamb both benefit from being served pink, with the added bonus of taking less time to cook. Pork and chicken need to be cooked through, but if you cut them into strips or flatten them into thinner pieces, they will cook much more quickly. The Marinated Mango Pork Medallions on page 149 are brimming with tangy flavour and take only 5–10 minutes to cook. Here, as in other dishes in the book, the meat is marinated quickly first, which is such an effective way to add instant flavour to a dish.

How you cook is as important as what you cook when it comes to speed. Cooking on the hob or under the grill generally takes less time than cooking in the oven – stir-frying in particular. You'll see that I've included a number of delicious stir-fry dishes, taking inspiration from Chinese and Thai cooking. For the TV series that accompanies this book, I visited London's Chinatown and watched chefs at work as they chopped up vegetables at lightning speed and stir-fried them in huge woks over a fiery heat. While I wouldn't advise cooking in this way at home (even if you are in a hurry!),

chopping vegetables into small pieces and stir-frying them over a high heat in a non-stick pan does help them to cook more quickly and ensures they stay crisp and full of flavour.

When it comes to quick cooking, Italy is hard to beat. I visited Rome for the TV programme and have included a number of Italian-inspired recipes in this book. Pasta is such a great store-cupboard stand-by – it's so fast to cook and can be paired with a whole range of delicious sauces. It goes beautifully with seafood and fish or with vegetables of different kinds. You could try the Spaghetti with Salmon, Chilli and White Wine on page 180 or the Tagliatelle with Mushrooms and Stilton on page 183 – an ideal dish for vegetarians. With their layers of delicious toppings, Italian-style bruschetta make the perfect lunch (see page 34). You'll find them in a chapter devoted to quick bites that could be used as snacks, nibbles, starters or light lunches, or presented as part of a larger spread. The Three Tapas on pages 45–6, for example, can be enjoyed on their own or served together Spanish-style for a casual meal with friends.

While stews generally rely on slow cooking, I've included a few speedier versions here, such as the Burgundy Chicken on page 132 and the Lamb Tagine on page 158. They still take some time to cook, but they are worth the effort. For *Quick Cooking*, I visited Marrakech, where I watched a family prepare a tagine in the traditional time-honoured way, each ingredient added to the dish in exactly the same order as it had been done for generations. Full of flavour from all the spices and other ingredients, my version can be cooked in much less time and still tastes delicious.

Classic dishes from around the world tend to incorporate lots of different spices, but I've discovered that you really don't need them all. Just buy a few key spices and stick to them – you'll find you use them again and again. That goes for other store-cupboard basics, too. There are certain items that are ideal for adding flavour quickly, such as roasted red peppers in oil, which provide a tasty alternative to roasting red peppers from scratch, or richly savoury miso paste – perfect for Asian-style soups and glazes.

A Little Bit of Planning

When it comes to making tarts and pies, shop-bought filo and puff pastry are so convenient and simple to use. Among the sweet dishes here, I've used filo for the Blackberry and Custard Money Bags on page 238 – something a bit different to serve your guests. If you're too busy to make your own lemon or orange curd, a good-quality shop-bought jar can be a real time-saver.

Be sure to read the label so you know they are made of pure ingredients – avoid additives. I've used one in the Limoncello Trifle on page 243, for example – a spectacular dish that takes only 15 minutes to assemble – as well as the moist and creamy Apple and Lemon Sandwich Cake on page 273. The Passion Fruit and Orange Cheesecake on page 233 is made without gelatine and also takes only 15 minutes to prepare.

As with savoury dishes, splitting things up into smaller quantities helps if you're in a hurry. The no-churn Rum and Raisin Ice Cream on page 234 is even quicker to prepare if you freeze it in ramekins rather than a large container, while the Piccoli Tiramisù on page 249 consist of individual small puddings that are quicker to set than the larger Italian classic on which they are based. For a teatime treat, you could try the Orange, Lemon and Lime Cupcakes on page 263 – speedier to bake than a full-sized cake but just as delicious – or the Scone Fruit Crown on page 270, which looks impressive but is so quick to cook (10–12 minutes in the oven) and perfect to serve a crowd.

Throughout the recipes, I've given tips on how to save time or make the preparation of a recipe more straightforward. I've also included advice on preparing ahead and freezing dishes where possible. For the TV series I visited a wide range of restaurants and eating places, but what struck me about all of them was how well organised they were. Thinking ahead is something of a mantra of mine as I strongly believe that it can really help, especially when you're busy. A little bit of forward planning makes all the difference.

Researching and putting together the dishes for this book has been a great pleasure. I do hope you enjoy making them and that you discover in the process that one is never too busy to knock up a nourishing and delicious meal. Once you get into the swing of it, you won't look back – I guarantee it. You'll soon be rustling up your own flatbreads, dips and speedy curries – much tastier and more satisfying than any convenience foods or takeaways!

Mary Berry

Light Bites and Tapas

Breakfast on the Go

Perfect to make the day before and leave in the fridge overnight ready to grab in the morning. Add 1 tablespoon of chopped hazelnuts to the oat mix, if you like. You can use any dried fruit that's in the store cupboard – dried cranberries would add a lovely colour, but raisins or chopped figs (left over from the Figgy Oat Squares on page 266) would be nice too.

SERVES 4 · PREP TIME: *10 minutes* · COOK TIME: *5 minutes, plus cooling*

a knob of butter
50g (2oz) porridge oats
1 tbsp sunflower seeds
1 tbsp pumpkin seeds
5 ready-to-eat dried apricots, chopped into tiny pieces
1–2 tbsp runny honey (to taste)
50g (2oz) blueberries
75g (3oz) raspberries
200g (7oz) Greek-style natural yoghurt (see note)

You will need clean, lidded jars, such as Kilner or jam jars.

Melt the butter in a small frying pan over a medium–high heat. Add the oats and seeds, stir together and fry for 2–3 minutes, until starting to toast. Remove from the heat, and add the apricots and honey, stirring well.

Set aside on a flat plate to cool down.

Divide the fresh fruit between the jars and press down slightly. Spoon the yoghurt on top and sprinkle with the cooled oat mixture (see note) in a deep layer. Cover with the lids and chill in the fridge until needed.

COOK'S NOTES
- Give the yoghurt a good stir before spooning out of its pot, as it can separate a little. Using a thick yoghurt means it will not become runny overnight.
- If the cooled oats have stuck together in large clumps on the plate, break them up into bite-sized pieces before adding to the yoghurt.

PREPARE AHEAD
Can be made the day before and kept in the fridge overnight.

FREEZE
Not suitable for freezing.

All-in-One Sausage and Egg Breakfast

An all-in-one breakfast dish to serve four hungry teenagers or indeed anyone with a hearty appetite! It's also a great way to cook breakfast in a hurry – with much less washing-up too. Perfect hangover food, or so I am told!

SERVES 4 · PREP TIME: *10 minutes* · COOK TIME: *30 minutes*

8 good-quality pork sausages
   (see note)
1 tbsp sunflower oil
2 large just-ripe tomatoes,
   quartered
250g (9oz) large field
   mushrooms, thickly sliced
4 large eggs
2 tbsp finely snipped chives

Preheat the oven to 200°c/180°c Fan/Gas 6.

Place the sausages in a large roasting tin, add the oil and toss together, then roast in the oven for about 15 minutes until the sausages are golden underneath.

Turn the sausages over, scatter with the tomatoes and mushrooms and season with salt and pepper. Return to the oven to cook for another 10 minutes.

Crack the eggs into the roasting tin and return to the oven for a further 4–5 minutes or until just set. Sprinkle with the chives and serve with buttered toast.

COOK'S NOTE
If you use chipolata or cocktail sausages, this dish will take even less time to cook – about 20 minutes in total.

PREPARE AHEAD
Best made and served at once.

FREEZE
Not suitable for freezing.

Gruyère and Chive Omelette

Surely the quickest of all meals and so economical too. It only takes about 3 minutes to make and uses mostly store-cupboard ingredients. You can swap the chives for fresh parsley if you prefer. Water is added to the beaten egg to make it a lighter omelette.

SERVES 1 · PREP TIME: *2 minutes* · COOK TIME: *5 minutes*

2 large eggs
a knob of butter
15g (½oz) Gruyère cheese, grated
2 tsp snipped chives

You will need a 20cm (8in) omelette pan (see note).

Break the eggs into a bowl. Add 2 teaspoons of water and some salt and pepper and beat together with a fork until well mixed.

Heat the omelette pan until extremely hot, add the butter and, when it is foaming, pour in the egg mixture and tilt the pan to swirl the mixture around the base.

Using a spatula or palette knife, push the nearest third of the egg mixture into the middle of the pan making ripples. Draw any uncooked egg towards you and repeat the ripples in the same direction. Once the base is just set but the top still slightly runny, sprinkle the cheese and chives over the half of the omelette furthest away from you and the handle.

When almost set, loosen the omelette around the edges with the spatula and fold the plain half over the portion with the cheese and chives, then flip over, away from you, on to a warmed plate. (If you find this tricky with the hot pan, just slide the folded omelette out of the pan on to a small plate and invert a plate over the top to turn it out more easily.)

Serve immediately with green leaves or a tomato salad.

COOK'S NOTE
Make sure your pan has a solid, flat base. Invest in a good-quality non-stick pan, if you can, as the cheaper ones can be thin and buckle quickly, meaning the omelette will not cook evenly.

PREPARE AHEAD
Best made and served at once.

FREEZE
Not suitable for freezing.

Smoked Mackerel Pâté

Quick, easy and perfect as a starter or a light lunch. You could switch the smoked mackerel for smoked salmon trimmings, if you prefer.

SERVES 4–6 · PREP TIME: *15–20 minutes, plus 1 hour chilling*

6 sprigs of flat-leaf parsley
1 bunch of spring onions,
    roughly chopped
45g (1½oz) butter, softened
180g (6oz) full-fat cream
    cheese
225g (8oz) smoked mackerel
    fillets, skinned (see note)
juice of 1 small lemon

You will need 4–6 small jars or ramekins or a small serving dish.

Place the parsley and spring onions in a food processor. Whizz until roughly chopped, then use a spatula to transfer to a mixing bowl. Add the butter to the processor and whizz for a minute until soft and fluffy, then add the cream cheese and briefly mix until well blended. Add the fish, lemon juice and plenty of freshly ground black pepper. Whizz until smooth, then spoon into the bowl with the parsley and spring onions. Mix well and check the seasoning, adding salt and more pepper if needed.

Spoon the pâté into the jars/ramekins or a serving dish and place in the fridge to chill for a minimum of 1 hour. Bring to room temperature for about 10 minutes before serving with griddled bread or Melba Toasts (see page 71).

COOK'S NOTE
Smoked mackerel fillets come in sealed packs, either plain or sprinkled with crushed peppercorns. For this recipe, it is best to use the plain variety.

PREPARE AHEAD
The pâté can be made up to a day ahead and kept in the fridge.

FREEZE
Not suitable for freezing.

Hot-Smoked Salmon and Avocado

Served on individual plates, this makes a speedy, smart first course that can be prepared ahead. Chargrilled artichoke hearts in oil are available from the supermarket in jars.

SERVES 6 · PREP TIME: *20 minutes* · COOK TIME: *30 minutes*

flesh of 2 ripe avocados, sliced into thin strips
juice of 1 lemon
1 × 60g bag of lamb's lettuce
4 chargrilled artichoke hearts in oil (from a jar), drained and halved
200g (7oz) hot-smoked salmon flakes (see note)
25g (7oz) mixed seeds (such as sunflower and pumpkin), toasted (see note)
fresh dill to garnish

FOR THE DRESSING
4 tbsp mayonnaise
100g (4oz) crème fraîche
1 tbsp tomato purée
1 tbsp hot horseradish sauce
2 tsp fresh lemon juice
2 tbsp chopped dill

Carefully toss the avocado in the lemon juice to prevent it from discolouring.

Mix together the ingredients for the dressing and season with salt and pepper. Set aside.

Divide the lamb's lettuce between six plates. Sit the artichoke halves and avocado slices on top of the lettuce and scatter over the flaked pieces of salmon. Sprinkle with the toasted seeds and add a little blob of the dressing. Top with the dill and serve the remaining dressing in tiny bowls alongside the salad plates.

COOK'S NOTES
· Hot-smoked salmon flakes are easy to buy and have a woody, earthy flavour that's very different from that of standard cold-smoked salmon.
· To toast seeds or pine nuts, heat a frying pan until hot and toast them for a couple of minutes. Shake the pan to toast evenly, and watch them like a hawk so they don't burn!

PREPARE AHEAD
The dressing can be made up to 3 days ahead and stored in the fridge. The salad, without the avocado, can be assembled up to 6 hours ahead and kept in the fridge too. Add the avocado just before serving.

FREEZE
Not suitable for freezing.

Pan-Fried Halloumi with Quick, Fresh Tomato Chutney

I have never been that keen on halloumi; I've always found it a bit squeaky – which is what happens when it is overcooked! However, pan-fried in breadcrumbs and served with this delicious fresh tomato chutney, it is now one of my favourite light dishes.

SERVES 4 · PREP TIME: *15 minutes* · **COOK TIME:** *20 minutes*

1 × 250g block of halloumi cheese
25g (1oz) plain flour
1 large egg, beaten
2 tbsp milk
50g (2oz) panko breadcrumbs
about 2 tbsp sunflower oil
lamb's lettuce leaves, to serve

FOR THE TOMATO CHUTNEY
1 tbsp olive oil
1 small red onion, finely chopped
1 garlic clove, crushed
350g (12oz) cherry tomatoes, cut into quarters
2 tbsp balsamic vinegar
2 tsp light muscovado sugar
6 mild piquant baby red peppers in oil (from a jar), drained and finely sliced
1 tbsp chopped basil

First make the chutney. Heat the oil in a small frying pan over a high heat. Add the onion and fry for 2–3 minutes until softened, then add the garlic and cook for a further minute. Tip in the tomatoes and stir over the heat, then add the vinegar, sugar and peppers and cook for 5–10 minutes, stirring occasionally, until the mixture has reduced and the tomatoes have softened but still retain their shape. Season with salt and pepper, add the basil and set aside to cool.

Cut the halloumi into eight thickish slices. Take three plates – add the flour to one and season with salt and pepper, add the beaten egg and milk to another and place the breadcrumbs in a third (see note). Toss the halloumi slices in the seasoned flour, then dip in the egg mixture and finally toss in the breadcrumbs until coated all over.

Heat the oil in a large frying pan over a high heat. Fry the breadcrumb-coated pieces of cheese for 2 minutes on each side until golden and crisp.

Serve with the chutney (see note) and a few lamb's lettuce leaves.

COOK'S NOTES
- Putting the flour, breadcrumbs and egg on plates or in shallow bowls makes it much easier (and less messy!) to coat the cheese.
- Keep any leftover chutney to spread on ciabatta or to add to a sandwich for a tasty, quick lunch.

PREPARE AHEAD
The chutney can be made up to 2 days ahead and stored in the fridge. The halloumi can be coated up to 6 hours ahead and kept chilled.

FREEZE
Neither the pan-fried halloumi nor the chutney is suitable for freezing.

Tomato and Avocado Bruschetta with Olive Tapenade

These are my new favourite lunch. If your ciabatta loaf is long and narrow, cut it on the diagonal to give a larger surface area to hold all the topping.

SERVES 6 · PREP TIME: *30 minutes* · **COOK TIME:** *4 minutes*

2 tbsp olive oil, plus extra for
    drizzling
1 garlic clove, crushed
6 thick slices of ciabatta loaf
flesh of 1 just ripe avocado,
    sliced widthways into strips
1 tbsp fresh lemon juice
2 ripe tomatoes, deseeded and
    sliced into strips
leaves of 1 small bunch of
    basil, some torn and some
    left whole to garnish
200g (7oz) buffalo mozzarella,
    torn into pieces

FOR THE TAPENADE (see note)
70g (2½oz) pitted black olives,
    drained if from a jar
3 tbsp sun-dried tomato paste
1 tsp runny honey
1½ tsp white wine vinegar

Measure all the tapenade ingredients into a mini food processor. Whizz until well chopped and the mixture forms a rough paste, then season with salt and pepper and set aside.

Heat a griddle pan or heavy-based frying pan until hot.

Mix the oil and garlic together in a bowl. Brush the ciabatta slices with the garlic oil and then chargrill or pan-fry the bread for 2 minutes on each side until brown and crispy.

Remove from the heat and spread the tapenade over the toasts.

Mix the avocado with the lemon juice, then arrange on the toasts, followed by the tomato strips, torn basil and mozzarella. Season well.

Drizzle with extra oil before serving, and garnish with the whole basil leaves.

COOK'S NOTE
You can use shop-bought tapenade to speed things up, though I find my homemade one makes the recipe extra special. Make double the amount, so you've extra for another day – place in a sterilised jar (see page 282) and store for 3–4 days in the fridge.

PREPARE AHEAD
Can be assembled up to an hour ahead – but no longer as the toasts will start to become soggy.

FREEZE
Not suitable for freezing.

Pan-Fried Spiced Falafel

Easy to make, these falafels are savoury fried patties – a mixture of chickpeas, onions and spices. Quick to cook, these are great as a snack or for lunch with a salad. They are delicious wrapped in flatbreads with tzatziki or hummus – try the Garlic Herb Flatbreads and Spiced Carrot Hummus on pages 38 and 41. Harissa paste is a mixture of roasted red peppers, chillies and spices. You'll find it in a jar in good supermarkets. Dried harissa seasoning is also available and can be found with the dried herbs and spices.

SERVES 4–6 · PREP TIME: *15 minutes* · COOK TIME: *4–6 minutes per batch*

plain flour, for coating
2 tbsp sunflower oil

FOR THE FALAFEL
1 bunch of coriander
1 bunch of spring onions
1 garlic clove, crushed
1 × 400g tin of chickpeas,
  drained and rinsed
  (see note)
finely grated zest of ½ lemon
1 tbsp harissa paste
2 heaped tsp ground cumin
1 tsp runny honey

Place the coriander, spring onions and garlic in a food processor and whizz until roughly chopped. Add the remaining falafel ingredients and whizz again until more finely chopped but still with a bit of texture. Season well with salt and pepper. If time allows, refrigerate for 15 minutes to firm.

Divide the mixture into ten pieces, then roll each piece into a ball and flatten slightly (see note). Scatter the flour on a plate and lightly roll each falafel in the flour to coat in a thin layer.

Heat the oil in a frying pan over a medium–high heat and fry the falafel in batches, adding more oil if needed, for 2–3 minutes on each side until golden and heated through. Transfer to a plate lined with kitchen paper and keep warm until ready to serve.

Serve warm with a dip or salad, such as the Beetroot, Red Onion and Feta Salad on page 88. The yoghurt sauce on page 152 would go nicely with this too.

COOK'S NOTES
· After rinsing, drain the chickpeas well and make sure they are not wet – dry them with kitchen paper, if necessary.
· Use some of the flour to dust your hands to stop the mixture sticking.

PREPARE AHEAD
Can be made up to 8 hours ahead and kept in the fridge.

FREEZE
Not suitable for freezing

Garlic Herb Flatbreads

The quickest of flatbreads to make and so versatile too. Perfect for dipping, try them with the Spiced Carrot Hummus on page 41, or fill with homemade falafel (see page 37) and salad, or your favourite cold meats and cheese as an alternative sandwich.

MAKES 6 · PREP TIME: *10 minutes* **· COOK TIME:** *30 minutes*

225g (8oz) plain flour, plus extra for dusting
2 tbsp olive oil, plus extra for frying
130ml (4½fl oz) warm water
2 garlic cloves, crushed
2 tbsp chopped parsley
1 tbsp chopped basil

Measure the flour, oil and water into a large bowl and add a good pinch of salt. Mix everything together with a table knife and then use your hands to bring the mixture together into a soft dough. Tip on to a floured work surface and knead for 4–5 minutes.

Flatten the dough into a circle, sprinkle over the garlic and herbs and then bring together into a ball again. Knead until the garlic and herbs are well incorporated (see note).

Divide into six even-sized balls, then use a rolling pin to roll each one out into a very thin circle on a floured work surface.

Heat a large frying pan until it's very hot (see note), then rub some oil into the pan using kitchen paper. Add one flatbread and fry for 2 minutes until it starts to puff up and turn lightly golden. Use a palette knife to flip over the flatbread and cook for another 2–3 minutes on the other side. Repeat with the remaining flatbreads, adding a little more oil to the pan if needed.

Serve warm with dips.

COOK'S NOTES
· If you like spiced flatbreads, add crushed spices to the dough too. Cumin or caraway seeds or chilli flakes would work well.
· For best results, the pan needs to be really hot before adding the first flatbread.

PREPARE AHEAD
Best made and served at once.

FREEZE
Not suitable for freezing.

Spiced Carrot Hummus

Hummus is always a favourite dip – why not try this slightly different spiced carrot version for a change?

2 smallish carrots (about 125g/4½oz in total), coarsely grated
1 × 400g tin chickpeas, drained and rinsed
2 garlic cloves, crushed
juice of ½ lemon
150ml (5fl oz) olive oil
2 tsp tahini
2 tsp harissa paste

Place all the ingredients in a food processor, season with salt and pepper and whizz until just smooth and creamy (see note).

Serve with crudités, pittas or other flatbreads, such as the Garlic Herb Flatbreads on page 38.

COOK'S NOTE
Do not over-whizz the mixture or the carrots and chickpeas will be too finely ground and may produce excess water, making the hummus too wet.

PREPARE AHEAD
Can be made up to 2 days ahead and kept, covered, in the fridge. Give it a good stir before serving.

FREEZE
Not suitable for freezing.

Three Tapas

These tapas can be put together speedily and, served together, are a wonderful way of presenting a range of delicious tastes and textures.

Roasted Cauliflower

SERVES 6 · PREP TIME: *5 minutes* · COOK TIME: *30 minutes*

1 large cauliflower, broken into small florets (about 500g/1lb 2oz prepared weight)
2 tbsp sunflower oil
1 tbsp paprika
2 tbsp finely grated Parmesan or vegetarian hard cheese

Preheat the oven to 200°C/180°C Fan/Gas 6.

Arrange the cauliflower florets in a roasting tin. Add the oil and paprika and toss together, then season well with salt and pepper. Roast in the oven for 25 minutes until tender and lightly browned at the edges.

Sprinkle over the Parmesan and roast for a further 5 minutes, then arrange in a bowl and serve immediately.

Garlic Mushroom Tapas

SERVES 6 · PREP TIME: *10 minutes* · COOK TIME: *10 minutes*

1 tbsp sunflower oil
400g (14oz) button mushrooms (white or chestnut), trimmed but left whole
a knob of butter
2 garlic cloves, crushed
½ tsp sweet smoked paprika
a squeeze of lemon juice
2 tbsp chopped flat-leaf parsley

Heat the oil in a large frying pan. Add the mushrooms and fry over a high heat for 4–5 minutes, stirring occasionally, until they start to release their liquid.

Add the butter and, when foaming, add the garlic, paprika and some salt and pepper. Continue to fry over a medium–high heat for another 4–5 minutes, giving the pan a shake every now and then, until the mushrooms are golden and any liquid has evaporated.

Add the lemon juice and parsley and serve at once.

Patatas Bravas

SERVES 6 · PREP TIME: *10 minutes* · COOK TIME: *30–40 minutes*

3 tbsp sunflower oil
750g (1lb 10oz) potatoes,
    peeled and cut into 2cm
    (¾in) dice
½ tsp sweet smoked paprika

FOR THE SAUCE
1 tbsp sunflower oil
1 small onion, finely chopped
1 garlic clove, crushed
½ tsp sweet smoked paprika
½ × 400g tin of chopped
    tomatoes
1 tbsp sun-dried tomato paste
    (see note)

Preheat the oven to 200°c/180°c Fan/Gas 6.

Measure the 3 tablespoons of sunflower oil into a large roasting tin and place in the oven to heat through for 5 minutes. Add the potatoes, paprika and some salt and pepper and toss together in the hot oil. Return to the oven and roast for 30–40 minutes, turning halfway through the cooking time, until golden and crisp.

Meanwhile, to make the sauce, heat the oil in a saucepan, then add the onion and garlic and fry for about 5 minutes over a medium heat. Stir in the paprika, followed by the tomatoes and tomato paste. Simmer for 5 minutes, stirring occasionally, until the sauce is reduced and thickened. Season with salt and pepper.

Arrange the roast potatoes on a serving plate, spoon over the sauce and serve with cocktail sticks.

COOK'S NOTE
Using sun-dried tomato paste gives a particularly rich flavour to the sauce for the Patatas Bravas.

PREPARE AHEAD
The cauliflower can be cut up into florets, ready for roasting, up to 2 hours ahead, while the sauce for the Patatas Bravas can be made 2–3 days in advance and stored in the fridge, then reheated to serve.

FREEZE
None of the tapas is suitable for freezing.

LIGHT BITES AND TAPAS

Artichoke-Stuffed Button Mushrooms

These are full of subtle flavour and look great too. They would also be lovely as a starter served on sourdough toast.

MAKES 25 · PREP TIME: *15 minutes* · COOK TIME: *15 minutes, plus cooling*

500g (1lb 2oz) button chestnut
    mushrooms
a knob of butter
100g (4oz) artichoke hearts in
    brine or oil (from a tin or
    jar), drained and finely
    chopped
2 tbsp mayonnaise
25g (1oz) mature Cheddar,
    finely grated
1 tbsp chopped parsley

Preheat the oven to 180°c/160°c Fan/Gas 4.

Remove the stalk from each mushroom and scoop out a little of the inside from where the stalk was attached.

Heat a large frying pan over a high heat and add the butter. When the butter is foaming, tip in the mushrooms. Cover the pan with a lid, reduce the heat to medium and fry for 3–4 minutes until all the liquid from the mushrooms has been released.

Remove the lid and cook for another 3–4 minutes until the liquid has evaporated (see note). The mushrooms should be tender but still firm. Transfer to a baking sheet, gill side up, and leave until cool enough to handle.

Mix all the remaining ingredients together in a bowl and season well with salt and pepper. Spoon a little of the mixture into the scooped-out hollow of each mushroom. Cook in the oven for 5–7 minutes until heated through.

Serve the mushrooms at once on small spoons as they are a little tricky to pick up otherwise.

COOK'S NOTE
Covering the pan with a lid quickly draws the liquid from the mushrooms. Driving it off afterwards with the lid removed seals in the flavour and ensures the mushrooms stay firm.

PREPARE AHEAD
Can be assembled up to 6 hours ahead and chilled until ready to cook in the oven to serve .

FREEZE
Not suitable for freezing.

New Potatoes with Blue Cheese and Chives

Think of potato wedges with blue cheese dip – but in canapé form. Bursting with flavour and very moreish!

MAKES ABOUT 15 • PREP TIME: *15 minutes* • COOK TIME: *25–35 minutes*

500g (1lb 2oz) baby new
    potatoes (see note)
1 tbsp olive oil
50g (2oz) Stilton or other blue
    cheese, coarsely grated
4 tbsp soured cream
4 tbsp snipped chives
paprika, for dusting

Preheat the oven to 200°C/180°C Fan/Gas 6.

Put the potatoes in a roasting tin, add the oil and some salt and pepper and shake until the potatoes are coated. Slide into the oven to roast for 25–35 minutes, depending on the size of the potatoes, until golden brown and tender.

Meanwhile, mash the cheese, soured cream and chives together in a small bowl and season.

Remove the potatoes from the oven and leave to cool slightly. Using a small sharp knife, slice halfway through each potato to make a little pocket. Put a teaspoonful of the cheese mixture into the gap and on top of each potato. Return to the oven for 5 minutes to heat through.

Arrange the filled potatoes on a platter and sprinkle with paprika. Serve warm.

COOK'S NOTE
Try to use potatoes that are all the same size so that they roast at the same rate.

PREPARE AHEAD
Can be assembled up to 4 hours ahead and heated through in the oven to serve.

FREEZE
Not suitable for freezing.

Red Pepper and Goat's Cheese Tapas

Perfect little bites and so quick to make – I often have them on a busy working day. Just pop them in the oven for a snack lunch. The goat's cheese that is best to use is sold in a thin roll wrapped in cellophane. It helps to slice it straight from the fridge. The jars of roasted red peppers are a great timesaver as the peppers are already skinned and deseeded. Do make sure they are well drained before adding to the baguette slices, so they don't make the bread soggy.

MAKES 20 · PREP TIME: *15 minutes* · COOK TIME: *8–10 minutes*

2 tbsp olive oil
1 part-baked baguette (see note)
1 × 200g goat's cheese log
3 rounded tbsp sun-dried tomato paste
150g (5oz) roasted red peppers in oil (from a jar), well drained and thinly sliced
25g (1oz) Parmesan, finely grated

Preheat the oven to 220°c / 200°c Fan / Gas 7, then line a large baking sheet with baking paper and brush with the oil (see note).

Cut the baguette into 1cm (½in) slices – you should get about 20 slices – and arrange them on the prepared baking sheet. Thinly cut the goat's cheese into the same number of slices.

Spread the sun-dried tomato paste over the baguette pieces. Top each with 3–4 strips of red pepper and a slice of goat's cheese, then sprinkle with Parmesan and season with salt and pepper.

Bake in the oven for 8–10 minutes, until golden and crisp. Serve warm.

COOK'S NOTES
· Part-baked loaves are a great store-cupboard standby, with a longer shelf-life than fresh baguettes, so you can buy them well in advance of using them.
· Brushing the baking paper with oil is quicker than brushing the underside of each slice of bread.

PREPARE AHEAD
Can be assembled up to 6 hours ahead and kept in the fridge before baking.

FREEZE
Not suitable for freezing.

Roasted Pepper and Ricotta Rolls

These are like tiny vegetarian sausage rolls – no meat in sight but just as delicious!
The rolls benefit from being chilled before baking, so if you have time, leave them
in the fridge for 10 minutes.

MAKES 24–30 · PREP TIME: *15 minutes* · COOK TIME: *15–18 minutes*

200g (7oz) roasted red peppers in oil (from a jar), drained and chopped
125g (4½oz) full-fat ricotta cheese
50g (2oz) Parmesan or pecorino cheese, grated
2 tbsp chopped basil
plain flour, for dusting
1 × 320g packet of ready-rolled all-butter puff pastry (see note)
1 egg, beaten

Preheat the oven to 200°c/180°c Fan/Gas 6 and line a large baking sheet with baking paper.

Place the peppers in a bowl and add the two cheeses and the basil. Mix together and season to taste with salt and pepper.

On a floured work surface, roll out the pastry to make it slightly thinner and to form a rectangle measuring about 25 × 48cm (10 × 19in). Brush the pastry with the beaten egg and cut it widthways into six strips each measuring about 8 × 25cm (3 × 10in).

Divide the pepper and cheese mixture into six and place a sixth of the mixture along the long edge of each pastry strip, leaving a 1cm (½in) border. Brush both long edges with beaten egg, then fold the pastry in half lengthways and press the long edges together to seal. Trim the edges using a sharp knife and then crimp with the back of a fork. Place the finished rolls in the fridge to chill as you make the others (see note on page 54).

Use a large sharp knife to slice each roll on the diagonal into 4–5 pieces, then place on the prepared baking sheet and brush with more beaten egg. Bake in the oven for 15–18 minutes until golden and cooked through. Serve warm.

COOK'S NOTES
· Using ready-rolled puff pastry is best, to save time; if you buy it in a block, be sure to roll it out thinly.
· The pastry is easiest to work with if you remove it from the fridge only 10 minutes before use.

PREPARE AHEAD
The finished rolls can be made up to a day ahead. Store in the fridge and reheat in the oven to serve.

FREEZE
The cooked rolls freeze well.

Mini Sausage Rolls with Thyme

These are so simple but will always be the first to go at a party. Making mini sausage rolls with ready-rolled puff pastry means that they are quicker to prepare and cook than the classic larger ones.

MAKES 30–36 · PREP TIME: *20 minutes* · COOK TIME: *12–15 minutes*

225g (8oz) pork sausage meat
50g (2oz) mature Cheddar, grated
2 tsp chopped thyme leaves
1 × 320g packet of ready-rolled all-butter puff pastry (see note on page 53)
1 egg, beaten
2 tbsp Dijon mustard
plain flour, for dusting

Preheat the oven to 220°C/200°C Fan/Gas 7 and line a large baking sheet with baking paper.

Place the sausage meat, cheese and thyme in a bowl and season with salt and pepper. Mash together with a fork until combined.

Roll out the pastry on a floured work surface so that it is slightly thinner and forms a rectangle measuring about 25 × 48cm (10 × 19in). Brush the pastry with the beaten egg and then cut it widthways into six strips each measuring about 8 × 25cm (3 × 10in).

Divide the sausage mixture into six even-sized portions, then roll each into a long sausage shape (see note) and place lengthways along one side of each pastry strip, leaving a 1cm (½in) border along that edge. Brush both long edges with beaten egg, then fold the pastry in half lengthways and press the long edges together to seal. Trim the edges using a sharp knife and then crimp with the back of a fork. Place the finished rolls in the fridge to chill as you make the others (see note).

Use a large sharp knife to slice each roll on the diagonal into 5–6 pieces. Place on the prepared baking sheet and brush with more beaten egg. Bake in the oven for 12–15 minutes until golden and cooked through. Serve warm.

COOK'S NOTES
· If the sausage-meat mixture is sticky and hard to handle, try wetting your palms before rolling it.
· The rolls benefit from being chilled before baking, so if you have time, leave them in the fridge for 10 minutes first.

PREPARE AHEAD
These can be made up to a day ahead. Store in the fridge and reheat in the oven to serve.

FREEZE
The cooked rolls freeze well for up to a month.

Brie, Chutney and Tomato Toasties

Tiny titbits of posh cheese on toast! Perfect to hand round with drinks. The thinner and more evenly everything is spread on the toast, the crisper it will be and you'll have a taste of all the toppings in each bite.

MAKES 16 · PREP TIME: *10 minutes* · COOK TIME: *5 minutes, plus resting*

2 slices of wholemeal bread, toasted
50g (2oz) ripe Brie, at room temperature (see note)
2 tsp mango or onion chutney
4 cherry tomatoes, halved and thinly sliced
1 tsp chopped parsley

Preheat the grill to high.

Spread each slice of toast with Brie right to the edges (see note), then spread the chutney over the cheese and top with the tomato slices, taking care to distribute them evenly. Season well with salt and pepper.

Place under the grill to cook for 2–3 minutes or until the cheese has melted and is lightly golden brown. Watch that the toast doesn't burn!

Leave for a few minutes before cutting each slice of toast into eight rectangles. Sprinkle with the parsley and serve warm.

COOK'S NOTES
· Take the Brie out of the fridge 10 minutes before using, as this will help it spread more easily.
· Make sure the whole slice of bread is well covered with the toppings so that the edges don't burn when it goes under the grill.

PREPARE AHEAD
Best made and served at once.

FREEZE
Not suitable for freezing.

Speedy Soups

Everyday Vegetable Soup

During the summer I usually eat salad for lunch, but for the rest of the year I have soup pretty much every day, and this is one of my favourites.

SERVES 6 · PREP TIME: *10 minutes* **· COOK TIME:** *20–25 minutes*

a large knob of butter
1 onion, sliced (see note)
2 carrots, sliced
2 parsnips, sliced
200g (7oz) butternut squash, peeled, deseeded and diced
1.4 litres (2½ pints) chicken or vegetable stock

Melt the butter in a large saucepan over a medium–high heat. Add the onion, carrots, parsnips and squash, and fry for 4–5 minutes, stirring frequently, until the vegetables are starting to soften. Season with salt and pepper.

Pour in the stock and bring to the boil, then reduce the heat, cover with a lid and simmer for about 15 minutes until the vegetables are tender.

Check the seasoning and serve hot.

COOK'S NOTE
You can replace the onion with sliced leeks, if you prefer.

PREPARE AHEAD
Can be made up to 2 days ahead and reheated.

FREEZE
Freezes well.

Fennel and Celeriac Soup

Smooth and velvety and using two of my favourite vegetables, this soup is really special. Full-fat milk gives a lovely rich flavour and is worth the extra calories!

SERVES 6 · PREP TIME: *5–10 minutes* · COOK TIME: *25–30 minutes*

1 tbsp olive oil
a knob of butter
1 onion, finely sliced
2 small fennel bulbs, core removed, finely sliced
700g (1lb 9oz) peeled celeriac, diced
1 litre (1¾ pints) chicken or vegetable stock (see note)
300ml (10fl oz) full-fat milk

Heat the oil and butter in a deep saucepan over a medium–high heat. When the butter has melted, add the onion and fennel and fry for 3–4 minutes until starting to soften. Add the celeriac and cook for 2–3 minutes, stirring occasionally, then pour in the stock and milk. Bring to the boil, then reduce the heat, cover with a lid and simmer for about 15 minutes or until the celeriac is tender.

Blend in a food processor or using a hand blender and season to taste with salt and pepper.

Serve hot with Melba Toasts (see page 71).

COOK'S NOTE
Use a good-quality stock to really enhance the flavour of this simple soup.

PREPARE AHEAD
Can be made up to a day ahead and reheated.

FREEZE
Freezes well.

Vegetable Miso Soup

A stock-based Japanese soup, quick and fresh. My version is made using vegetables, but you could add chicken or tofu. If you like a little heat, add a sprinkle of dried chilli flakes before serving.

SERVES 4–6 · PREP TIME: *10 minutes* · COOK TIME: *10–15 minutes*

4 tbsp white miso paste
1.4 litres (2½ pints) vegetable
   or chicken stock
2 tsp grated fresh root ginger
1 bunch of spring onions
   (about 6–8), thinly sliced
2 tbsp soy sauce
1 tbsp light muscovado sugar
200g (7oz) shiitake
   mushrooms, sliced
   (see note)
½ small savoy cabbage,
   shredded (see note)

TO SERVE
leaves of ½ bunch of
   coriander, roughly chopped
1–2 tsp toasted sesame oil

Measure the miso paste into a bowl. Gradually add 150ml (5fl oz) of the chicken stock and whisk together until smooth.

Pour the remaining stock into a large saucepan and place over a high heat. Add the miso mixture and whisk until smooth, then tip in the grated ginger and bring to the boil. Add the spring onions, soy sauce, sugar, mushrooms and cabbage, then simmer for 5–10 minutes, until the vegetables are tender.

Season to taste with salt and pepper and spoon into bowls. Sprinkle over the coriander leaves and a few drops of the toasted sesame oil. Serve hot.

COOK'S NOTES
· Shiitake mushrooms add a lovely depth of flavour; if you can't find them fresh, you could use dried, but you'll need to soak them first.
· Savoy cabbage has a wonderful flavour and texture, though you could use pointed spring cabbage instead.

PREPARE AHEAD
The soup can be made a day ahead and kept in the fridge. It will separate and become cloudy; give it a good stir and reheat gently before adding the coriander leaves and sesame oil to serve.

FREEZE
Not suitable for freezing.

Vichyssoise

Such a delicious classic recipe, often known simply as leek and potato soup. Traditionally it is served chilled, though I prefer it hot. This recipe is for Jo, my lovely make-up artist for TV and photo shoots – I could not do without her. She had never heard of Vichyssoise, then tasted it in a restaurant and said we should put it in this book!

SERVES 6 · PREP TIME: *10 minutes* · COOK TIME: *25 minutes*

a large knob of butter
1 onion, chopped
3 large leeks, sliced
500g (1lb 2oz) potatoes, peeled and diced
600ml (1 pint) chicken or vegetable stock
200ml (7floz) milk
100g (4oz) crème fraîche
1 tbsp snipped chives, to garnish

Melt the butter in a large saucepan over a high heat. Add the onion and leeks and fry for a few minutes. Reduce the heat, cover with a lid and cook for about 5 minutes or until softened. You want the leeks to steam rather than to brown.

Add the potatoes and cook, with the lid on, for another 2–3 minutes. Pour in the stock, cover again with the lid and bring to the boil, then reduce the heat and simmer for about 15 minutes until the vegetables are soft.

Remove from the heat, stir in the milk and crème fraîche and season with salt and pepper. Blend until completely smooth using a food processor or hand blender.

Serve hot garnished with the chives (see note), or in chilled bowls if serving cold.

COOK'S NOTE
You could top the soup with the Paprika Croûtons on page 70 or add some crumbled blue cheese.

PREPARE AHEAD
Can be made up to 2 days ahead and reheated.

FREEZE
The blended soup freezes well.

Smoky Red Pepper and Bean Soup

A hearty, warming soup with a lovely rich flavour and a nice kick from the chilli.
You could add 50g (2oz) of pan-fried thin chorizo strips, if you like.

SERVES 4–6 · PREP TIME: *15 minutes* · COOK TIME: *20 minutes*

2 tbsp olive oil

2 banana shallots, sliced

1 large carrot, finely diced

1 red pepper, deseeded and
finely diced

½ fresh red chilli, deseeded
and finely diced

1 garlic clove, crushed

1 tsp sweet smoked paprika

2 tbsp tomato purée

1 tbsp plain flour

1.2 litres (2 pints) hot chicken
stock (see note)

1 × 400g tin of cannellini
beans, drained and rinsed

2 tbsp chopped parsley,
to serve

Place the oil in a saucepan over a high heat. Add the shallots, carrot and red pepper and fry for 3–4 minutes, stirring occasionally. Add the chilli and garlic and fry for another 30 seconds. Sprinkle in the paprika and add the tomato purée. Stir well for 1 minute.

Sprinkle over the flour and stir it in. Gradually add the hot stock, stirring all the while, then tip in the cannellini beans and season with salt and pepper. Bring to the boil, then reduce the heat, cover with a lid and simmer for about 15 minutes or until the vegetables are tender.

Serve hot sprinkled with the parsley.

COOK'S NOTE
Use vegetable stock, if you prefer, to make a
vegetarian soup.

PREPARE AHEAD
Can be made up to 2 days ahead and reheated
to serve.

FREEZE
The basic soup, without the beans, freezes well.
Add the beans when reheating.

Tomato and Tarragon Soup with Mozzarella Croûtes

Tomato is usually paired with basil, but tarragon goes beautifully with it too. Sourdough bread is ideal for making the croûtes as it really adds to the flavour.

SERVES 6 · PREP TIME: *10 minutes* · **COOK TIME:** *25–30 minutes*

2 tbsp olive oil, plus extra to serve (optional)
2 large onions, sliced
2 garlic cloves, crushed
2 × 400g tins of chopped tomatoes (see note)
4 tomatoes, chopped
2 tbsp tomato purée
500ml (18fl oz) vegetable or chicken stock
1 tbsp caster sugar
1 tbsp chopped tarragon leaves
3 tbsp double cream

FOR THE CROÛTES
2 slices of sourdough, or other good-quality bread
1 tbsp olive oil
100g (4oz) mozzarella, coarsely grated

Heat the 2 tablespoons of olive oil in a large saucepan over a medium heat, add the onions and fry for about 10 minutes, stirring occasionally, until just softened and lightly golden brown. Add the garlic and fry for another 15 seconds. Add the tinned and fresh tomatoes, the tomato purée, stock and sugar, and bring to the boil. Reduce the heat, cover with a lid and simmer for about 15 minutes.

Add the tarragon and cream, then season well with salt and pepper and blend until smooth using a hand blender.

Meanwhile, preheat the grill to medium.

Toast the slices of bread on one side under the grill. Turn them over, brush the untoasted sides with the olive oil and cover with the mozzarella. Place back under the grill to cook for about 5 minutes or until the cheese has melted. Use a small pastry cutter to stamp out rounds to make 12–18 croûtes (see note).

Spoon the soup into bowls and top each bowl with croûtes, and a drizzle of olive oil if you like, before serving.

COOK'S NOTES
· Use good-quality tinned tomatoes, as they will greatly enhance the colour of the soup.
· Stamping out rounds is a quick way of making croûtes, but you could use slices of thin baguette.
· If you don't have time to make croûtes, just top the soup with some grated mozzarella.

PREPARE AHEAD
The soup can be made up to a day ahead and reheated. The croûtes can be prepared (up until topping with cheese) up to 4 hours ahead and then cooked under the grill to serve.

FREEZE
The soup freezes well without the croûtes.

Rather Special Cauliflower Soup

Cauliflowers are as cheap as chips! And they make excellent soup. Gruyère would work well here in place of Cheddar. Don't throw away the cauliflower leaves; keep all except the toughest outer ones and slice and use them in a stir-fry.

SERVES 8 · PREP TIME: *15 minutes* · COOK TIME: *20 minutes*

1 medium cauliflower
25g (1oz) butter
1 large onion, roughly chopped
25g (1oz) plain flour
1 litre (1¾ pints) hot vegetable or chicken stock (see note)
50g (2oz) mature Cheddar, grated
100ml (3½fl oz) double cream

Remove the outer leaves of the cauliflower and discard (see recipe introduction). Using a sharp knife, cut the cauliflower into quarters, then pull or cut off the florets, trim off the tough ends of the remaining stalk and dice the rest. Gather up any smaller florets and the tiny pieces that have fallen off and put these into a bowl to add texture later. Keep the larger florets and any of the softer, younger leaves for the main part of the soup.

Melt the butter in a pan over a high heat. Add the onion, then cover the pan, lower the heat and gently cook for about 5 minutes. Remove the lid, raise the heat and boil off any excess liquid, then sprinkle in the flour and stir until combined. Cook for a minute. Gradually pour in the hot stock, stirring so there are no lumps, and bring to the boil. Add the larger cauliflower florets and the diced stalk, then season with salt and pepper and simmer for about 10 minutes, or until tender.

Remove the pan from the heat and whizz with a hand blender until smooth (see note). Return to the heat, check the seasoning, add the reserved florets and small bits of cauliflower and bring to the boil. Cover with a lid and boil for 2–3 minutes until just cooked. Add the Cheddar and cream and stir until the cheese has melted.

Check the seasoning and serve hot.

COOK'S NOTES
· Using hot stock means the soup is quicker to make.
· If the soup is a little thick, add a bit more stock to thin it down.
· If you don't have a hand blender, you can liquidise the soup in a food processor.

PREPARE AHEAD
The basic soup can be made up to 2 days ahead. Store in the fridge and reheat, adding the reserved florets, Cheddar and cream to serve.

FREEZE
The basic soup freezes well for up to a month.

Chicken Noodle Soup

Hearty, healthy and good for the soul. It's really important to use a good-quality chicken stock as this will give the soup the best flavour. If you're using leftover chicken from a roast, you could save the carcass to make a homemade stock (see page 281).

SERVES 4 · PREP TIME: *10 minutes* · COOK TIME: *15 minutes*

a knob of butter

1 onion, thinly sliced

1 carrot, halved and thinly sliced

1.7 litres (3 pints) good-quality, hot chicken stock

50g (2oz) fine egg noodles (about 2 small nests – see note)

100g (4oz) cooked chicken, thinly shredded into long strips

4 spring onions, sliced on the diagonal

Melt the butter in a large saucepan. Add the onion and carrot and fry for 3–4 minutes over a high heat. Pour in the stock, cover with a lid and bring to the boil, then reduce the heat and simmer for about 5 minutes.

Break the noodles into small pieces, or keep them longer if you like, then add to the soup with the chicken. Cover the pan and simmer for another 5 minutes or until the noodles are just cooked.

Add the spring onions and season with salt and pepper to serve.

COOK'S NOTE
If you don't have egg noodles, use rice noodles or spaghetti instead.

PREPARE AHEAD
Make the base of the soup up to 4 hours ahead, adding the chicken and vermicelli to serve.

FREEZE
The base of the soup, with the chicken added, can be frozen. Add the vermicelli when reheating, simmering the soup until they are soft.

Quick Toppings and Toasts for Soup

Adding a topping to a soup can turn it into something extra-special. Just that little bit of finesse to complete the dish can make all the difference. Croûtons are so easy to make at home; these Paprika Croûtons would work well with a creamy celery soup or the Vichyssoise on page 62. See also the Mozzarella Croûtes on page 64. The Melba Toasts may seem old-fashioned but they are such a treat to serve, adding lovely crunch, and they are very easy and quick to make.

Paprika Croûtons

SERVES 6 · PREP TIME: *5 minutes* · COOK TIME: *6–8 minutes*

2 medium slices of stale white
    bread, crusts removed
2 tbsp sunflower oil
1 tsp paprika (see note)

Preheat the oven to 200°C/180°C Fan/Gas 6.

Cut the bread into squares or batons about 1 × 5cm (½ × 2in) in size. Put them into a bowl and toss in the oil and paprika until coated. Season with salt and pepper, then arrange in a single layer on a baking sheet. Bake in the oven for 6–8 minutes, turning them halfway through the cooking time, until crisp and golden.

Cheese and Tomato Croûtes

MAKES ABOUT 16 · PREP TIME: *5 minutes* · COOK TIME: *5 minutes*

½ thin baguette
sun-dried tomato paste,
    for spreading
25g (1oz) Gruyère, grated

Preheat the grill to high.

Slice the baguette into about 16 slices and toast one side under the grill. Spread the untoasted side with a little sun-dried tomato paste and then top with the grated cheese. Pop under the grill to cook for 3–4 minutes or until just melted.

Melba Toasts

MAKES 16 · PREP TIME: *5 minutes* · COOK TIME: *8–10 minutes*

2 medium slices of
white bread

Preheat the oven to 200°c/180°c Fan/Gas 6.

Toast the bread in a toaster until lightly golden. Cut off the crusts while still warm and slice the toast in half horizontally to make four thin slices. Leave to cool a little.

Slice each slice into four triangles, place on a baking sheet and bake for 8–10 minutes, or until golden brown and the edges have curled up. Leave to cool before serving.

Cheesy Melba Toasts

MAKES 16 · PREP TIME: *6–8 minutes* · COOK TIME: *8–10 minutes*

2 medium slices of
white bread
olive oil, for brushing
25g (1oz) Parmesan,
finely grated

Preheat the oven to 200°c/180°c Fan/Gas 6.

Toast the bread in a toaster until lightly golden. Cut off the crusts while still warm and slice the toast in half horizontally to make four thin slices. Leave to cool a little.

Brush the cut side of each slice of toast with a little olive oil, then season with salt and pepper. Sprinkle with the Parmesan before cutting each slice into triangles.

Place on a baking sheet and bake for 8–10 minutes, or until golden brown and the edges have curled up. Leave to cool before serving

COOK'S NOTE
You could swap the paprika in the croûtons for other flavourings or spices, such as sesame seeds, grated Parmesan, ground cumin or chilli flakes, depending on the soup you are serving them with.

PREPARE AHEAD
Make the Melba Toasts and Cheese and Tomato Croûtes up to 6 hours in advance; pop the croûtes under the grill just before serving. The croûtons can be made up to 3 days ahead and stored in an airtight container.

FREEZE
None of these are suitable for freezing.

Salads and Grains

Cabbage and Fennel Slaw

Slaw, as it is now trendily called, does not have to be thick with mayonnaise. You can vary the dressing to make it fresh and healthy. For this recipe I have included a quick lemon and caper dressing made with yoghurt rather than mayonnaise. It is quite runny, which helps to give the cabbage and fennel a good coating.

SERVES 6 · PREP TIME: *15 minutes*

2 fennel bulbs, trimmed

1 small pointed green cabbage, very finely shredded (see note)

2 spring onions, trimmed and sliced

FOR THE DRESSING

100g (4oz) Greek-style natural yoghurt

1 tbsp grainy mustard

juice of 1 small lemon

2 tbsp capers, rinsed and chopped

1 tsp sugar (or to taste)

Measure all the dressing ingredients into a large bowl, season with salt and pepper and whisk together until combined. Set aside.

Cut the fennel bulbs in half, remove and discard the core, then very thinly slice into strips (see note). Add to the bowl with the dressing. Tip in the cabbage and spring onions, then season and mix together until everything is well coated.

Serve in a pretty bowl or platter.

COOK'S NOTES

· Pointed green cabbage, sometimes called sweetheart cabbage, is a little softer than a classic white cabbage, so slightly less crunchy, which I prefer for this recipe.

· There's no right or wrong way to slice fennel. Depending on the shape of the bulb, it can be cut horizontally or lengthways, and you may like to keep the leafy fronds for the garnish.

PREPARE AHEAD

Make up to 4 hours ahead and keep in the fridge.

FREEZE

Not suitable for freezing.

Red Cabbage and Apple Coleslaw with Walnuts

A crunchy slaw with a tangy crème fraîche sauce. To save time, slice the vegetables with a food processor, if you have one. If you're not keen on raw onion, soak it first – this will reduce its potency. Pat it dry before adding it to the salad with the other ingredients. Otherwise, you could use half the amount: it adds a lovely piquancy to offset the creamy dressing so don't just leave it out.

SERVES 6–8 · PREP TIME: *15 minutes*

juice of 1 large lemon
1 red eating apple, cored and diced into bite-sized chunks
150g (5oz) full-fat crème fraîche (see note)
4 tbsp mayonnaise (see note)
1 tbsp Dijon mustard
75g (3oz) walnut pieces, toasted (see note)
1 tbsp chopped parsley
½ small red cabbage, thinly sliced
2 carrots, grated (see note)
1 small red onion, thinly sliced

Pour the lemon juice into a large bowl. Add the apple pieces and toss in the juice, then add the crème fraîche, mayonnaise, mustard, nuts and parsley. Season with salt and pepper and mix well.

Stir in the cabbage, carrots and onion and toss everything together to coat in the dressing. Cover and chill in the fridge until ready to serve.

COOK'S NOTES
· Using crème fraîche and shop-bought mayonnaise means that this is a very quick sauce to make; just remember to season it well.
· Walnut pieces are often cheaper than whole shelled walnuts and save you the time of chopping them.
· If you're short of time, there's no need to peel the carrots – just give them a good wash before grating.

PREPARE AHEAD
Can be made up to a day ahead and stored in the fridge. If the dressing separates, toss the slaw again to mix before serving.

FREEZE
Not suitable for freezing.

Moroccan Summer Salad

Grains are so popular and great as part of a healthy salad. Broad beans are also called fava beans and add texture and flavour, as well as making the salad a bit more substantial. You could use ready-cooked sachets of grains and pulses to make it even speedier – you'll need two 250g sachets.

SERVES 4–6 • PREP TIME: *15 minutes* • COOK TIME: *15 minutes, plus optional cooling*

100g (4oz) bulgur wheat
100g (4oz) three-colour quinoa
    blend (red, white and black)
1 × 300g tin of broad or fava
    beans, drained and rinsed
3 spring onions, finely sliced
¼ red onion, finely sliced
½ fresh red chilli, deseeded
    and finely chopped
2 celery sticks, finely chopped
leaves from 1 large bunch of
    mint, chopped
1 large bunch of parsley,
    chopped

FOR THE DRESSING
juice and finely grated zest
    of 1 lemon
1 tbsp white wine vinegar
1 garlic clove, crushed
6 tbsp olive oil

Cook the bulgur wheat and quinoa according to the packet instructions until just tender (see note).

Drain any excess liquid and combine the two in a large serving bowl, then stir in the broad or fava beans. Add the spring onions, red onion, chilli and celery, season well with salt and pepper and stir everything together.

Combine the dressing ingredients in a jug or bowl, then season and mix well. Pour the dressing over the salad, toss together and then mix in the herbs to serve.

If the salad is still warm, set aside until cold before adding the herbs (see note).

COOK'S NOTES
· Cook the bulgur wheat and quinoa in the same pan to save on washing up – just add the one that needs less time after starting to cook the first.
· If you add the herbs while the grains are still warm, they may lose their bright green colour.

PREPARE AHEAD
Can be made up to 8 hours ahead; add the dressing up to 2 hours before serving.

FREEZE
Not suitable for freezing.

Nutty Wholemeal Couscous Salad

Like many grain-based dishes, couscous salad can be a little bland without lots of added flavourings, provided here by the peppers, spring onions and parsley, while the pistachios give a lovely texture. The baby red peppers come in a jar; they give a hit of sweet, piquant flavour and are also great stuffed with a little cream cheese as hors d'oeuvres alongside olives. Wholemeal couscous is less refined and contains a bit more fibre, but standard couscous would also work well. Whichever you use, it's the ultimate grain for speedy cooking – made from steam-dried semolina, it just needs to be rehydrated in stock, as here, or boiling water. This would go well with the Lamb Tagine on page 158.

SERVES 4–6 · PREP TIME: *10 minutes* · COOK TIME: *2–3 minutes, plus soaking*

300g (11oz) wholemeal
    couscous
4 tbsp olive oil
450ml (15fl oz) boiling
    vegetable or chicken stock
100g (4oz) shelled pistachios
1 large bunch of parsley,
    chopped
1 bunch of spring onions,
    sliced
12 mild piquant baby red
    peppers in oil (from a jar),
    drained and sliced
juice of 1½ lemons

Place the couscous in a large bowl, add 1 tablespoon of the oil and mix to coat the grains. Pour over the boiling stock, stir and cover the bowl with cling film. Leave for 10 minutes until soft, then fluff up the grains with a fork to break up any that have clumped together.

Heat a frying pan until hot. Toast the nuts for 2–3 minutes, stirring constantly, until golden brown (see note). Roughly chop and add to the couscous.

Add the parsley, spring onions, peppers, lemon juice and the remaining oil to the bowl. Season to taste with salt and pepper and stir well.

Serve cold or warm.

COOK'S NOTE
Toasting the pistachios is so worth doing as it brings out the flavour. Watch them like a hawk so they don't burn!

PREPARE AHEAD
Can be made up to 6 hours ahead and kept in the fridge.

FREEZE
Not suitable for freezing.

Superfood Salad

A meal in itself – this is full of so much fresh flavour, varied texture and overall goodness!

SERVES 4–6 · PREP TIME: *15 minutes* · COOK TIME: *25 minutes*

100g (4oz) long-grain brown rice (see note)
1 × 400g tin of green lentils, drained and rinsed (see note)
1 large carrot, grated
½ fresh red chilli, deseeded and finely diced
1 bunch of spring onions, sliced
1 bunch of parsley, chopped
250g (9oz) cooked beetroot, diced (see page 281)

FOR THE DRESSING
2 tbsp white wine vinegar
4 tbsp olive oil
1 tsp caster sugar

Cook the rice in boiling water for about 25 minutes or according to the packet instructions, then drain and refresh in cold water. Drain well once again.

Place the cooked rice and tinned lentils in a large bowl with the carrot, chilli, spring onions and parsley. Season with salt and pepper and mix together well.

Combine the dressing ingredients together in a jug, then pour over the salad and toss to mix. Spoon into a serving bowl and scatter over the beetroot to serve.

COOK'S NOTES
· Using pouches of ready-cooked rice will make this even quicker to prepare.
· You can substitute 100g (4oz) dried lentils, if you prefer. Cook them according to packet instructions.

PREPARE AHEAD
Can be made up to 6 hours ahead and stored in the fridge. Bring up to room temperature and add the beetroot to serve.

FREEZE
Not suitable for freezing.

Squash, Goat's Cheese and Quinoa Salad

This salad contains more squash than quinoa, and with fresh herbs and a little goat's cheese, it can be enjoyed as a meal in itself or as a side salad.

SERVES 4–6 · PREP TIME: *15 minutes* · COOK TIME: *15 minutes*

50g (2oz) quinoa
1 medium butternut squash,
    peeled, deseeded and cut
    into 2cm (¾in) cubes
½ fresh red chilli, deseeded
    and diced
4 tbsp chopped parsley
3 tbsp chopped mint leaves
3 spring onions, thinly sliced
200g (7oz) hard goat's cheese,
    crumbled into large pieces
    (see note)
juice of 1 lemon
4 tbsp olive oil

Cook the quinoa according to the packet instructions.

Meanwhile, bring a pan of salted water to the boil and cook the squash cubes for about 10 minutes or until tender (see note). Drain and then season with salt and pepper.

Arrange the warm squash cubes on a large serving plate, then scatter over the cooked quinoa with the chilli, herbs, spring onions and goat's cheese. Mix the lemon juice and oil together, then season and pour over the salad.

COOK'S NOTES
· Hard goat's cheese is perfect for this recipe as it is more delicate in flavour than the soft variety.
· If you prefer, you can roast the squash for even more flavour – see page 202.

PREPARE AHEAD
The salad can be assembled up to 4 hours ahead; drizzle over the dressing just before serving.

FREEZE
Not suitable for freezing.

Spiced Lentils with Pickled Ginger

When testing recipes for a new book, there is often one absolute favourite
and for me this was it. I ate it every day for a whole week!

SERVES 4 · PREP TIME: *10 minutes* · COOK TIME: *40 minutes*

200g (7oz) dried Puy lentils
(see note)
2 tbsp olive oil
1 large onion, chopped
2 garlic cloves, crushed
¼ tsp ground cumin
2 tbsp balsamic vinegar
2 tbsp soy sauce
2 tbsp tomato ketchup
3 tbsp sweet chilli sauce
40g (1½oz) pickled sushi
ginger (from a jar), drained
and chopped
1 small bunch of coriander,
chopped

Cook the lentils in boiling water for about 30 minutes or according
to the packet instructions, then drain well.

Heat the oil in a frying pan. Fry the onion for 5 minutes over a
high heat to brown it (taking care not to let it burn), then cover
with a lid, reduce the heat and cook for another 5 minutes or until
soft. Remove the lid and cook further to drive off any excess liquid,
then add the garlic and fry for another 30 seconds.

Add the cumin seeds, vinegar and soy sauce. Reduce the liquid
over a high heat for 15 seconds, then add the remaining
ingredients and stir until heated through.

Serve either hot with Chargrilled Aubergines (see page 218)
or cold with other salads.

COOK'S NOTE
If Puy lentils aren't available, substitute any green
lentils. You can buy Puy lentils ready-cooked in
sachets – for speed use two packs instead of the
200g (7oz) dried lentils. You could also use two tins
of green lentils.

PREPARE AHEAD
Can be made up to 8 hours ahead and reheated
to serve.

FREEZE
Not suitable for freezing.

Beetroot, Red Onion and Feta Salad

Arrange on a platter, rather than in a bowl – this looks so attractive, as well as fresh and delicious. You can buy pine nuts ready toasted, but it's just as easy (and cheaper) to toast your own.

SERVES 4–6 · PREP TIME: *10 minutes, plus marinating*

500g (1lb 2oz) small cooked
    beetroots, peeled and sliced
    (see note)
50g (2oz) pine nuts, toasted
100g (4oz) feta, crumbled
1 tbsp chopped parsley

FOR THE DRESSING
1 tbsp caster sugar
2 tsp Dijon mustard
2 tbsp white wine vinegar
2 tbsp olive oil
½ small red onion, thinly
    sliced

Arrange the beetroot slices on a large serving platter.

To make the dressing, mix the sugar, mustard, vinegar and oil together in a bowl and season well with salt and pepper. Add the onion and leave for about 10 minutes to marinate, then pour the onion mixture over the beetroot.

Adjust the seasoning, if needed, and scatter with the pine nuts, feta and parsley to serve.

COOK'S NOTE
It's nice to buy raw beetroot and cook it yourself (see page 281) but if you don't have time, shop-bought cooked beetroot is fine – just make sure you don't buy the beetroot that is stored in vinegar.

PREPARE AHEAD
The basic salad can be assembled up to 4 hours ahead and kept in the fridge. Crumble over the feta and sprinkle with parsley just before serving.

FREEZE
Not suitable for freezing.

Layered Tomato, Bean and Avocado Salad

This is a little salad to take on a picnic or to bring with you to work or school on a busy day. A convenience salad – just like you would buy in the supermarket but fresher and bursting with flavour. If you can't find cos, use two Little Gems instead.

SERVES 4 · PREP TIME: *20 minutes* · COOK TIME: *5 minutes*

100g (4oz) green beans, trimmed
1 large cos lettuce, shredded
flesh of 1 extra-large ripe avocado, roughly chopped
1 bunch of spring onions (about 8 or 9), finely sliced
12 cherry tomatoes (on the vine), cut into quarters (see note)
2 tbsp chopped basil leaves

FOR THE DRESSING
juice of ½ lemon
3 tbsp olive oil
½ tsp caster sugar
½ small garlic clove, crushed

You will need four clean lidded jars or airtight plastic containers.

Cook the green beans in boiling salted water for 4 minutes, then drain and refresh in cold water. Drain again and dry well on kitchen paper before slicing finely.

Divide the shredded lettuce between the four jars or plastic containers. Grind some black pepper on top of the leaves and spoon in the avocado.

In a separate bowl, mix together the spring onions, tomatoes and sliced cooked beans and season with salt and pepper. Toss in two-thirds of the chopped basil leaves.

Mix all the dressing ingredients together in a jug. If you are eating the salad within the next couple of hours (see Prepare Ahead), pour the dressing over the tomato mixture, then spoon the dressed tomatoes and beans on top of the avocado and sprinkle with the remaining basil before covering with the lids.

COOK'S NOTES
· For a more filling salad, you could spoon a little cooked bulgur wheat, couscous or quinoa into the bottom of the jar.
· Tomatoes on the vine are more expensive but worth paying a little more for, as the flavour is sweet and intense. For this recipe use the smallest ones that you can find.

PREPARE AHEAD
Layer and dress the salad up to 2 hours ahead, or layer it up to 6 hours ahead but keep the dressing separate. The avocado may discolour if not dressed, but the flavour won't be impaired.

FREEZE
Not suitable for freezing.

Asparagus, Feta, Pea and Olive Salad

Peas are often a forgotten vegetable when it comes to salads, but they give great flavour and colour and are so easy to use straight from the freezer. This has a hint of Greece from the feta and black olives and would make a great vegetarian main or a side dish for a barbecue.

SERVES 4–6 · PREP TIME: *15 minutes* · COOK TIME: *5 minutes*

150g (5oz) frozen petits pois
12 asparagus spears, woody
   ends removed (see note)
90g (3½oz) rocket leaves
100g (4oz) pitted black olives,
   drained if from a jar
200g (7oz) feta, crumbled into
   large chunks

FOR THE DRESSING
2 tsp Dijon mustard
2 tsp white wine vinegar
6 tbsp olive oil
½ fresh red chilli, deseeded
   and finely chopped
1 tsp caster sugar

Put a saucepan of salted water on to boil. When boiling, add the petits pois and cook for 3 minutes. Remove with a slotted spoon and refresh in a bowl of cold water before draining well (see note). Return the pan of water to the boil and add the asparagus. Boil for 2–3 minutes until al dente, then drain and refresh in cold water.

Scatter the rocket in a flat serving dish. Sprinkle the cooked peas over the top and arrange the asparagus spears. Scatter with the olives and feta and season with salt and pepper.

In a small bowl, mix the ingredients for the dressing together and pour over the salad. Serve immediately.

COOK'S NOTES
· No need to spend time trimming the asparagus – a quick bend of the stalk near the woody end and it should snap and break in just the right place.
· Make sure the peas and asparagus are really well drained after refreshing so no water is added to the salad.

PREPARE AHEAD
Can be assembled up to 4 hours ahead, without the feta. Store in the fridge, then add the feta and dress to serve. The dressing can be made up to 5 days ahead and kept in a jar in the fridge.

FREEZE
Not suitable for freezing.

Crab and Crayfish Salad with Fresh Mango

Full of fresh flavour, this is great to serve a crowd in the summer months. Mix it up by using melon instead of mango, or try a fruity or sweet cider vinegar in the dressing.

SERVES 6 · PREP TIME: *15 minutes*

100g (4oz) lamb's lettuce
2 Little Gem hearts, cut widthways into thick slices
250g (9oz) mango flesh, diced
1 cucumber, peeled, halved lengthways, deseeded and sliced into crescents
200g (7oz) cooked white crabmeat (see note)
120g (4½oz) peeled cooked crayfish tails (see note)
1 small bunch of chives, snipped

FOR THE DRESSING
8 tbsp olive oil
1 tbsp white wine vinegar
juice of 1 large lime
1 tbsp sweet chilli sauce

Scatter both types of lettuce over a large platter and add the diced mango and cucumber slices.

Arrange the crabmeat in six piles on top of the salad, then top each pile with an equal serving of crayfish tails. Sprinkle with the chives and season with salt and pepper.

Whisk all the dressing ingredients together in a jug or bowl. Pour over the salad just before serving.

COOK'S NOTES
· White crabmeat is easy to buy; if you particularly like the brown meat, add a little of that too.
· If you can't get hold of crayfish tails, use peeled cooked prawns instead.

PREPARE AHEAD
The salad can be prepared up to 4 hours ahead and dressed just before serving.

FREEZE
Not suitable for freezing.

Quick Salad Dressings

Classic French Dressing

MAKES ABOUT 125ML (4FL OZ) • PREP TIME: *5 minutes*

1 tbsp Dijon mustard
1 tsp caster sugar (or to taste)
6 tbsp olive oil
2 tbsp white wine vinegar

Measure all the ingredients into a bowl and mix with a balloon whisk until combined. Season to taste with salt and freshly ground black pepper.

Lemon Pesto Dressing

MAKES ABOUT 125ML (4FL OZ) • PREP TIME: *10 minutes*

2 tbsp Dijon mustard
2 tbsp Classic Basil Pesto (see page 190) or shop-bought pesto
juice of 1 lemon
4 tbsp olive oil
2 tsp caster sugar (or to taste)

Place all the ingredients in a bowl and mix well with a balloon whisk. Season to taste with salt and freshly ground black pepper.

Balsamic Dressing

MAKES ABOUT 125ML (4FL OZ) • PREP TIME: *5 minutes*

2 tsp Dijon mustard
1 tsp caster sugar (or to taste)
6 tbsp olive oil
2 tbsp balsamic vinegar

Measure all the ingredients into a bowl and mix with a balloon whisk until combined. Season to taste with salt and freshly ground black pepper.

Easy Caesar Dressing

MAKES ABOUT 200ML (7FL OZ) · PREP TIME: *5 minutes*

¼ garlic clove, crushed
2 tbsp white wine vinegar
½ tsp Dijon mustard
2 tsp olive oil
6 tbsp mayonnaise
25g (1oz) Parmesan or
    vegetarian hard cheese,
    finely grated
1 tsp caster sugar (or to taste)

Place the garlic, vinegar, mustard and oil in a bowl and mix with a balloon whisk until smooth. Add the mayonnaise, cheese, sugar and 3 tablespoons of water and whisk again to combine. Season to taste with salt and freshly ground black pepper.

Tomato and Basil Dressing

MAKES ABOUT 150ML (5FL OZ) · PREP TIME: *10 minutes*

4 tbsp olive oil
1 shallot, finely chopped
3 ripe tomatoes, deseeded and
    finely chopped
2 tbsp torn basil leaves
juice of 1 lemon
1 tsp caster sugar (or to taste)

Place all the ingredients in a bowl and mix with a balloon whisk until combined. Season to taste with salt and freshly ground black pepper.

COOK'S NOTE
For an easy way of making and storing a salad dressing, simply measure the ingredients into a clean jam jar, then close with a lid and shake to mix.

PREPARE AHEAD
The Classic French Dressing and Balsamic Dressing can be made a few days ahead. The remaining dressings, all of which use fresh ingredients, can be made up to 2 days in advance and stored in the fridge.

FREEZE
None of these dressings is suitable for freezing.

SALADS AND GRAINS

Fish

Miso Cod

This delicious, flavoursome cod uses miso, a classic Japanese paste made from soya beans, sea salt and koji (a mould used to ferment the beans), which can be found in the Asian aisle of a supermarket or in a health-food store. If the fillets are chunky rather than the flatter kind, they may need a minute longer under the grill.

SERVES 6 · PREP TIME: *10 minutes* **· COOK TIME:** *10–12 minutes*

sunflower oil, for greasing
2 tbsp brown miso paste
2 tbsp sweet chilli sauce
juice of ½ lemon
1 tsp sesame oil
1 tsp light muscovado sugar
6 × 150g (5oz) cod fillets, skinned
3 tbsp sesame seeds, toasted (see note)

Preheat the grill to high and grease a baking sheet with the sunflower oil.

Place the miso paste and sweet chilli sauce in a bowl with the lemon juice, sesame oil and muscovado sugar and mix together well.

Put the cod fillets on the prepared baking sheet and season with salt and pepper. Spoon some of the miso mixture on to each fillet, spreading it right to the edges.

Place under the grill for about 10–12 minutes, until the cod is cooked through and opaque and the topping forms a golden glaze.

Sprinkle over the sesame seeds and serve with rice or noodles and stir-fried pak choi.

COOK'S NOTE
Using ready-toasted sesame seeds would make this dish even quicker to prepare.

PREPARE AHEAD
The miso topping can be mixed up to a day ahead.

FREEZE
Not suitable for freezing.

Haddock, Leek and Dill Filo Tarts

A cross between a fish pie and a quiche, these little tarts would be ideal for a starter or for a light lunch.

MAKES 8 · PREP TIME: *20 minutes* · COOK TIME: *25 minutes*

FOR THE FILLING
30g (1oz) butter
1 leek, sliced
30g (1oz) plain flour
300ml (10fl oz) hot milk
50ml (2fl oz) white wine
1 rounded tsp grainy mustard
225g (8oz) undyed smoked
    haddock fillet, skinned and
    cubed (see note)
50g (2oz) mature Cheddar,
    finely grated
1 tbsp chopped dill
1 egg, hardboiled, peeled and
    roughly chopped

FOR THE PASTRY CASES
2 sheets of filo pastry
    (each measuring about
    30 × 34cm / 12 × 13in)
25g (1oz) butter, melted, plus
    extra for greasing

You will need two four-hole Yorkshire pudding tins. Preheat the oven to 220°C / 200°C Fan / Gas 7 and brush the holes with melted butter.

Melt the 30g (1oz) of butter in a saucepan. Add the leek, then cover with a lid and sweat over a medium heat for 5 minutes, stirring occasionally, until tender.

When the leek is soft, sprinkle in the flour and stir over the heat for 10 seconds. Add the hot milk and continue to stir until thickened. Pour in the wine and allow the sauce to boil, stirring all the while, until quite thick.

Add the mustard and haddock, reduce the heat and simmer, stirring occasionally, for about 8 minutes or until the fish is just cooked. Try not to break the fish up too much when you stir the sauce. Season well with salt and pepper and remove from the heat. Stir in the cheese, dill and egg.

Meanwhile, brush the sheets of filo with the melted butter. Cut one of the sheets into eight squares. Lay one square on top of another at an angle, then push this into one of the prepared holes of the Yorkshire pudding tin. Repeat with the other squares, then repeat with the remaining pastry. Scrunch up the pastry edges to add a bit of height to the pastry cases. Cook in the oven for 6–8 minutes until crisp and golden.

Spoon the hot filling into the cooked pastry cases and serve with a simple green salad.

COOK'S NOTES
- Buy undyed smoked haddock rather than the bright yellow kind.
- Filo makes a perfect tart case – it's so easy to work with.

PREPARE AHEAD
The pastry can be prepared and cooked up to 6 hours ahead. Make the filling and fill the pastry cases when you are ready to serve.

FREEZE
Not suitable for freezing, though any leftover pastry can be frozen (if it hasn't been frozen already).

Sea Bass en Papillote
with Courgette Ribbons

This is a delicate way to cook fish – and so easy too. Just remember to seal the foil parcels tightly so that the steam doesn't escape during cooking. The finished dish is best served simply with a few tiny new potatoes – Jersey Royals, if they're in season.

SERVES 4 · PREP TIME: *10 minutes* · COOK TIME: *15 minutes*

5 knobs of butter
4 sea bass fillets, skin on
(see note)
4 sprigs of thyme
4 tbsp white wine
3 large courgettes, cut into
thin ribbons using a
vegetable peeler
2 tsp chopped thyme leaves
juice of ½ lemon
freshly grated nutmeg

Preheat the oven to 200°C / 180°C Fan / Gas 6. Place four large squares of foil – each big enough to wrap one fish fillet well – on a work surface and place a smaller square of baking paper in the centre of each piece of foil (see note).

Place a knob of butter in the middle of each square. Lay a sea bass fillet on top of the butter, skin side down, and season well with salt and pepper. Add one sprig of thyme to each fillet, followed by a tablespoonful of wine. Fold over the paper and foil to make a parcel, turning over the edges to seal each one tightly. Place on a baking sheet and bake in the oven for 10–12 minutes. The parcels may puff up slightly during cooking.

Meanwhile, melt the remaining knob of butter in a very hot frying pan. Add the courgette ribbons and quickly stir-fry for 2 minutes until just wilted but still with a little bite. Add the thyme leaves, lemon juice and grated nutmeg to taste. Season well and divide between four plates.

Open the parcels, remove the sea bass and place on top of the courgettes. Peel off and discard the skin from each fillet and pour over any juices to serve.

COOK'S NOTES
· Keeping the skin on during cooking helps the sea bass fillets to retain their shape. It's also easier to remove the skin after cooking when it is soft. (I only serve fish with the skin on when it is pan-fried.)
· Look out for the double-sided foil with a baking paper backing; it will mean you don't need to spend time cutting out paper squares.

PREPARE AHEAD
The sea bass fillets can be prepared and wrapped in the foil parcels, ready to cook, up to 4 hours ahead.

FREEZE
Not suitable for freezing.

Ginger Teriyaki Salmon

Quick, simple and impressive-looking. Use thin, sustainably caught salmon fillets cut from the centre of the fillet, or swap with trout fillets if you like.

SERVES 4 · PREP TIME: *10 minutes, plus marinating* · COOK TIME: *5 minutes*

4 × 120g (4½oz) thin salmon fillets, skin on (see note on page 112)
2 tbsp sunflower oil
a small knob of butter
1 spring onion, sliced, to garnish

FOR THE MARINADE

¼ fresh red chilli, deseeded and finely chopped
juice of ½ lime
3 tbsp soy sauce
1 stem ginger bulb, very finely chopped (see note)
2 tbsp ginger syrup (from the stem ginger jar)
1 garlic clove, crushed

Place all the marinade ingredients in a shallow dish and mix well. Lay the salmon, flesh side down, in the marinade and spoon over the sauce to coat the fillets well. Leave for about 20 minutes or as long as time allows.

Heat a large frying pan until hot, then add the oil and butter. Season the fillets with salt and pepper and then fry them, flesh side down, over a high heat for about 2 minutes. Turn over and fry for a further 3 minutes, spooning the remaining marinade over the fillets as they cook, until the salmon is just cooked through and the sauce has thickened to a syrupy glaze.

Arrange the fillets on a platter or on individual plates, removing the skin, if preferred, then spoon over the sauce from the pan. Garnish with the sliced spring onion and serve with rice or stir-fried vegetables.

COOK'S NOTE
Stem ginger comes in syrup in a jar – not to be confused with crystallized ginger, also sold in a jar.

PREPARE AHEAD
Can be marinated in the fridge up to 6 hours ahead.

FREEZE
The cooked dish is not suitable for freezing. The raw fillets can be frozen with their marinade and cooked once defrosted.

Poached Salmon with Fragrant Flageolet Beans

This recipe is perfect for an al-fresco supper on a summer's evening. Don't expect punchy flavours, though – this is a refined and delicate dish.

SERVES 4 · PREP TIME: *10 minutes* · COOK TIME: *15 minutes*

1 tbsp white wine vinegar
1 small bunch of parsley, stalks reserved and leaves chopped
juice of 1 lemon
4 × 120g (4½oz) thin salmon centre-cut fillets, skin on (see note)
2 tbsp olive oil
2 shallots, finely chopped
1 garlic clove, crushed
2 × 400g tins of flageolet beans, drained and rinsed
a large knob of butter

TO GARNISH
½ lemon, cut into thin slices
4 parsley sprigs

Measure 600ml (1 pint) of water into a shallow saucepan, then add the vinegar, parsley stalks and half the lemon juice. Season with salt and pepper. Sit the salmon fillets in the liquid, skin side up. Bring to the boil and cook for 1 minute, then reduce the heat to a low simmer, cover with a lid and poach for about 5 minutes, or until the fish is just cooked – the flesh should turn an opaque pink all the way through.

Use a fish slice to transfer the fillets to a plate, then carefully peel off the skin and discard. Reserve 4 tablespoons of the poaching liquid. Cover the fillets with foil to keep warm.

Meanwhile, heat the oil in a large frying pan, tip in the shallots and gently fry over a low heat for about 2 minutes to soften. Add the garlic and fry for 15 seconds. Add the beans, remaining lemon juice and reserved poaching liquid and stir until combined and hot. Simmer for 2–3 minutes, then stir in the butter, chopped parsley leaves and some salt and pepper.

Divide the beans between four plates. Sit a salmon fillet on top of each and garnish with a lemon slice and a sprig of parsley. Serve with a green salad or some roasted cherry tomatoes on the vine.

COOK'S NOTES
- Leaving the skin on the salmon keeps it moist during cooking; if the skin is removed when the fish is warm, it will come off in one smooth piece. Choose long thin fillets for a more refined presentation.
- Any leftovers are good served cold the next day as a salad – lightly flake the salmon and mix into the beans.

PREPARE AHEAD
You can prepare the beans up to 4 hours ahead and reheat to serve.

FREEZE
Not suitable for freezing.

Prawn and Pollock Oaty Herb Crumble

Think fish pie with a crusty topping of breadcrumbs, oats and herbs rather than mashed potato. You can use cod or pollock – whichever you prefer.

SERVES 6 · PREP TIME: *20 minutes* · COOK TIME: *35 minutes*

50g (2oz) butter

50g (2oz) plain flour

450ml (15fl oz) hot milk

3 tbsp full-fat mayonnaise

2 tsp Dijon mustard

1 tbsp chopped dill

2 tsp snipped chives

juice of ½ lemon

50g (2oz) Cheddar, grated

650g (1lb 7oz) pollock, skinned and cut into 3cm (1¼in) cubes

200g (7oz) peeled raw king prawns, deveined

FOR THE TOPPING

175g (6oz) fresh white breadcrumbs

50g (2oz) porridge oats

100g (4oz) butter, melted

1 tbsp chopped fresh dill

1 tbsp snipped chives

50g (2oz) Cheddar, grated

Preheat the oven to 200°C/180°C Fan/Gas 6 and grease a fairly shallow 1.7-litre (3-pint) ovenproof dish.

Measure the butter into a wide-based saucepan and gently heat until melted. Add the flour and whisk for 30 seconds, then pour in the hot milk, whisking until the sauce is smooth and has thickened.

Add the mayonnaise, mustard, herbs, lemon juice and cheese and stir in well. Add the pollock and prawns and gently simmer for 2 minutes until the prawns just start to turn pink. Season with salt and pepper, then spoon into the ovenproof dish.

Mix all the topping ingredients together and season. Sprinkle over the dish in an even layer, then place on a baking sheet to catch any drips. Bake in the oven for about 25 minutes, or until bubbling around the edges, heated through and lightly golden and crisp on top. Serve with peas or a green vegetable.

COOK'S NOTE

Deveining prawns can be a faff. Leave in the vein if you're short of time. It isn't harmful, just tastier without.

PREPARE AHEAD

Make up to 8 hours ahead, adding the topping just before cooking. You could bake the completed dish in advance and then reheat.

FREEZE

Freezes well without the crumble topping, though you could freeze this separately and sprinkle over before cooking.

King Prawn and Broccoli Stir-Fry with Black Bean Sauce

A lovely, quick dish for a midweek meal. If you can't find oyster mushrooms, use chestnut mushrooms instead. Black bean sauce is fermented black or yellow soya beans.

SERVES 4 · PREP TIME: *10 minutes* · COOK TIME: *8 minutes*

2 tbsp sunflower oil
2 large shallots, very thinly sliced
2cm (¾in) knob of fresh root ginger, peeled and thinly sliced (see note)
1 fresh red chilli, deseeded and thinly sliced
350g (12oz) peeled raw king prawns, deveined (see note below and on page 113)
250g (9oz) broccoli, broken into tiny florets
150g (5oz) oyster mushrooms, thickly sliced
6 tbsp black bean sauce
2 tbsp dark soy sauce
juice of ½ lemon

Heat a large frying pan or wok until very hot. Add the oil, shallots, ginger and chilli and stir-fry over a high heat for 30 seconds. Push the vegetables to one side of the pan, then season the prawns with salt and pepper and add them to the centre of the pan. Fry for about 2 minutes until starting to turn pink. Tip in the broccoli and mushrooms, toss together using two spatulas and fry for 2–3 minutes.

Mix the black bean sauce, soy sauce and lemon juice together in a bowl. Add to the pan and toss everything together well. Stir-fry for another 2 minutes until the prawns are cooked and the broccoli is just tender but still crunchy.

Serve piping hot on its own or with rice or noodles.

COOK'S NOTES
· To peel a small knob of root ginger, which can be a bit tricky to handle, take a teaspoon and scrape away the skin – it will come off easily.
· Using raw prawns makes all the difference to this dish; if you use cooked prawns, they can become rubbery and lose their flavour.

PREPARE AHEAD
Best made and served immediately.

FREEZE
Not suitable for freezing.

Pan-Fried Scallops with Leeks and Tarragon

Scallops are quite a luxury but are quick to cook and a real treat for that special occasion. Serving the coral – the bright orange roe attached to each scallop – is a personal choice. Some people are not so keen on its texture but it is easy to cut off.

SERVES 4 · PREP TIME: *5 minutes* · **COOK TIME:** *10–15 minutes*

2 tbsp oil
2 knobs of butter
2 medium leeks, thinly sliced
1 garlic clove, crushed
150ml (5fl oz) white wine
150ml (5fl oz) double cream
1 tbsp finely chopped tarragon leaves
2 tbsp chopped parsley, plus extra to garnish (optional)
12 large king scallops (with or without the corals)
½ lemon, cut into wedges, to serve

Heat 1 tablespoon of the oil and a knob of butter in a wide, shallow saucepan. Add the leeks and stir over a high heat for 1 minute. Cover with a lid, reduce the heat and simmer for about 8 minutes, stirring occasionally, until the leeks are tender.

Remove the lid and increase the heat again, then add the garlic and fry for 10 seconds. Pour in the wine and boil until reduced by half. Add the cream and stir over the heat until reduced and the sauce has thickened slightly. Season with salt and pepper and add the chopped herbs.

Heat a large frying pan until very hot and season the scallops. Place the remaining oil in the pan, then add the scallops and fry over a high heat on each side for 1–1½ minutes (depending on how thick they are). When you have turned the scallops over, add the remaining knob of butter and baste the scallops well (see note).

Divide the leek mixture between four plates and arrange three scallops on top of each one. Sprinkle with parsley, if you like, and serve with the lemon wedges.

COOK'S NOTES
· To cook the scallops well, make sure the frying pan is very hot before you add them: they need to sizzle as soon as they touch the pan.
· Use a large knob of butter, so there is plenty to baste the scallops as they cook on their second side.

PREPARE AHEAD
Best made and served immediately.

FREEZE
Not suitable for freezing.

Quick Sauces for Fish

Chilli, Garlic and Tomato Sauce

SERVES 2 · PREP TIME: *5 minutes* · COOK TIME: *5 minutes*

2 tbsp olive oil
1 garlic clove, crushed
½ fresh red chilli, deseeded
    and finely diced
1 large just-ripe tomato,
    skinned, seeds removed
    and chopped (see note)
juice of ½ lemon

Heat the oil in a small frying pan over a medium heat. Add the garlic and chilli and fry for 1 minute. Add the chopped tomato and fry for another 1–2 minutes until softened. Remove from the heat and add the lemon juice, then season to taste with salt and freshly ground black pepper.

Serve with a firm white fish like cod or pollock.

Butter, Lemon and Dill Sauce

SERVES 4 · PREP TIME: *5 minutes* · COOK TIME: *5 minutes*

75g (3oz) butter
juice of 1 lemon
1 heaped tsp chopped dill

Melt the butter in a frying pan over a high heat until foaming. Stir in the lemon juice and then remove from the heat, add the dill and season to taste with salt and freshly ground black pepper.

Serve with a delicate flat fish such as sole or plaice.

Cold Herb Sauce

SERVES 4 · PREP TIME: *5 minutes*

200g (7oz) crème fraîche
½ tsp Dijon mustard
2 tbsp snipped chives
1 tbsp chopped tarragon leaves
1 tbsp chopped basil leaves
fresh lemon juice (to taste)

Measure the crème fraîche, mustard and herbs into a bowl, stir together well and season to taste with lemon juice, salt and freshly ground black pepper.

Serve with cold poached salmon.

COOK'S NOTE

To skin the tomato for the Chilli, Garlic and Tomato Sauce, cut a cross in the top, cover with boiling water, then leave to stand for a couple of minutes, drain and rinse in cold water. The skin should peel away easily.

PREPARE AHEAD

The Chilli, Garlic and Tomato Sauce can be made up to 2 days ahead, stored in the fridge and reheated to serve. The Butter, Lemon and Dill Sauce is best made and served immediately. The Cold Herb Sauce can be made a day ahead and stored in the fridge.

FREEZE

The sauces are not suitable for freezing.

Poultry and Game

Spiced Chicken Lettuce Cups

Delicious as an easy light lunch or as a starter. Eat them with your hands off a sharing platter or individual plates. If chicken mince is unavailable, use turkey mince instead.

SERVES 4–6 · PREP TIME: *10 minutes* **· COOK TIME:** *20–25 minutes*

2 tbsp sunflower oil

500g (1lb 2oz) raw minced chicken

1 red pepper, deseeded and finely diced

100g (4oz) button mushrooms, finely chopped

1 bunch of spring onions (about 6–8), finely chopped

1 tsp grated fresh root ginger

½ fresh red chilli, deseeded and finely diced

2 tbsp hoisin sauce

1 tbsp soy sauce

3 tbsp sweet chilli sauce

12 larger leaves from 2 Little Gem lettuces, washed and dried

juice of ½ lemon

2 tbsp chopped coriander

100g (4oz) crème fraîche (optional)

Heat the oil in a large frying pan over a high heat. Add the minced chicken and fry for 4–5 minutes, breaking up the mince using a wooden spoon, until starting to brown. Add the red pepper, mushrooms, spring onions, ginger and chilli and fry for 4–5 minutes until beginning to soften. Add the hoisin, soy and sweet chilli sauces and give everything a good stir so the mince is well coated. Continue to fry over a high heat until the mixture is fully cooked and quite dry, about 10 minutes. Season with salt and pepper and set aside to cool a little.

Arrange the 12 lettuce leaves, face up, on a serving plate, balancing them carefully so they are ready to be filled.

Add the lemon juice and coriander to the chicken and toss together. Spoon the mixture into the lettuce leaf cups and finish with a teaspoon of crème fraîche, if using.

Fill the leaves just before serving, so that the chicken is warm.

COOK'S NOTE
For speedy cooking, slice all the veggies in a food processor and pulse until roughly chopped into small pieces.

PREPARE AHEAD
The spiced mince can be made up to a day ahead and stored in the fridge. Just heat through to serve. Wash and dry the lettuce leaves in advance.

FREEZE
Not suitable for freezing.

Glazed Coriander Chilli Chicken

This flavoursome dish can be on the table in about 30 minutes and was inspired by a wonderful meal at a friend's house. A perfect weekday family dinner, served hot with minted new potatoes and a rocket and tomato salad.

SERVES 4 · PREP TIME: *10–15 minutes* · COOK TIME: *20 minutes*

4 tbsp sweet chilli sauce
juice and finely grated zest
    of 1 lime
5cm (2in) knob of fresh root
    ginger, peeled and grated
    (see note on page 114)
2 tbsp olive oil
1 small bunch of coriander,
    finely chopped
4 skinless and boneless
    chicken breasts

Preheat the oven to 200°c / 180°c Fan / Gas 6.

Measure the chilli sauce into a small bowl, add the lime juice and zest, ginger, olive oil and coriander and mix well.

Slice each chicken breast in half lengthways, then cover with cling film (or place in a freezer bag – see note) and use a rolling pin to bash to about 1.5cm (⅝in) thick (see note) to tenderise. Remove the cling film, season with salt and pepper and place in a large, shallow roasting tin, leaving lots of space around each breast.

Spoon over the sauce so that each breast is well coated, then roast in the oven for about 20 minutes until lightly golden and cooked through.

Remove the chicken and set aside. The juices can be served as a sauce: deglaze the tin with a little hot water, and pour over the chicken to serve.

COOK'S NOTES
· Using a freezer bag instead of cling film when you bash the chicken is a little less fiddly and you can reuse the bag for the other chicken breasts.
· Tenderising the chicken allows it to cook more quickly and gives a larger surface for coating with the sauce.

PREPARE AHEAD
If there is time, marinate the chicken in the sauce, in a bowl in the fridge, for up to 6 hours, ready to bake and serve.

FREEZE
The marinated raw chicken freezes well.

Chicken and Asparagus Fricassée

A speedy, French-inspired stew with fresh herbs and that king of green vegetables – asparagus. Oyster mushrooms are tender and therefore best kept in large pieces so they retain their charm. If they're not available, another exotic mushroom, such as shiitake, will work well, as will standard closed-cup or chestnut mushrooms.

SERVES 4 · PREP TIME: *10 minutes* · COOK TIME: *20 minutes*

3 tbsp olive oil

250g (9oz) oyster mushrooms, halved

4 skinless and boneless chicken breasts (about 150g/5oz each), sliced into thick pieces (see note)

1 small leek, sliced

1 garlic clove, crushed

150ml (5fl oz) white wine

150ml (5fl oz) double cream

200g (7oz) asparagus spears, stalks sliced into rounds and tips reserved

1 tbsp chopped mint leaves

1 tbsp chopped basil leaves

Heat 1 tablespoon of the oil in a large frying pan. Add the mushrooms, season with salt and pepper and fry over a high heat for 3–4 minutes until golden and any liquid has evaporated. Remove from the heat and set aside.

Heat another tablespoon of oil in the pan, season the chicken pieces and fry over a medium–high heat for 4–6 minutes until just cooked. Remove from the heat and set aside.

Add the remaining oil to the pan and gently fry the leek for 3–5 minutes until softened. Add the garlic to the leek and fry for 30 seconds. Pour in the wine and boil for 2–3 minutes to reduce by half, then stir in the cream and cook for another minute or so to reduce slightly – it will be a thin sauce.

Add the fried chicken pieces and mushrooms to the pan and simmer for a few minutes until heated through and the chicken is fully cooked, with no traces of pink in the middle.

Meanwhile, cook the asparagus in boiling salted water for 2–3 minutes, then drain and add to the chicken with the herbs. Season to taste and serve piping hot with potatoes.

COOK'S NOTE
Chicken mini fillets would save time as they cook quickly and do not need slicing. (You can keep the chicken breasts whole, if you prefer, but they will take longer to cook.)

PREPARE AHEAD
Can be made without the asparagus up to a day ahead. Reheat and then stir in the freshly cooked asparagus.

FREEZE
The cooked dish can be frozen without the asparagus.

Korma-Style Chicken Curry

This is my version of one of the nation's favourite curries. It's a little fiddly to remove the pods of the cardamom seeds, but you then get all the flavour and none of the green husk left in the curry sauce when serving. Give the pods a quick bash with a rolling pin, or use a pestle and mortar, and they will split easily so you can pick the seeds out.

SERVES 4–6 · PREP TIME: *10 minutes* **· COOK TIME:** *30 minutes*

5 skinless and boneless chicken breasts, sliced into thin strips
3 tbsp sunflower oil
2 onions, thinly sliced
2 garlic cloves, crushed
½ fresh red chilli, deseeded and finely chopped
2 tbsp medium curry powder
1 tsp ground cumin
10 green cardamom pods, crushed to remove the seeds (see recipe introduction)
450ml (15fl oz) chicken stock (see page 281)
125g (4½oz) ground almonds
2 tbsp mango chutney
juice of ½ lemon
200g (7oz) full-fat natural yoghurt
coriander leaves, to garnish

Season the chicken pieces with salt and pepper.

Heat a large, deep non-stick frying or sauté pan until piping hot and add 2 tablespoons of the oil. Quickly fry the chicken for 4–6 minutes until sealed and slightly golden. (You may need to cook the chicken pieces in batches if they don't fit in your pan in a single layer.) Remove with a slotted spoon and set aside.

Add the remaining oil to the pan with the onions, garlic and chilli and fry over a medium–high heat for 10 minutes, or until the onions are golden brown (see note). Add the spices and fry for another minute, stirring well to coat the onions. Stir in the stock, ground almonds and mango chutney, then bring to the boil and allow to bubble for 2–3 minutes.

Return the chicken to the pan and stir in. Reduce the heat, cover with a lid and simmer for about 5–7 minutes, until the chicken is cooked through.

Stir in the lemon juice and the yoghurt, check the seasoning and serve with boiled or steamed rice and garnished with coriander leaves.

COOK'S NOTE
Make sure the onions are golden as this will add to the colour of the sauce.

PREPARE AHEAD
Can be made up to a day ahead but leaving out the yoghurt. Reheat and stir in the yoghurt to serve.

FREEZE
Freezes well without the yoghurt.

Dry-Roasted Chicken Tikka

The marinade forms a paste that coats the chicken and, after roasting, gives it a rich, spicy flavour. The chicken is dry-roasted but you can serve it with a sauce if you prefer – see the variation below.

SERVES 6 · PREP TIME: *10 minutes, plus marinating* · COOK TIME: *30–35 minutes*

6 chicken thighs on the bone,
    skin on (see note)
6 chicken drumsticks, skin on
fresh coriander leaves,
    to garnish (optional)

FOR THE MARINADE
250g (9oz) Greek-style natural
    yoghurt
2cm (¾in) knob of fresh root
    ginger, peeled and grated
2 garlic cloves, crushed
juice of ½ lemon
2 tsp garam marsala
1 tsp ground turmeric
2 tsp tomato purée
1 tsp curry powder
1 heaped tsp mango chutney

Line a large baking sheet with baking paper (see note).

Place all the marinade ingredients in a bowl, season with salt and pepper and mix well until combined.

Score the skin of the chicken pieces and arrange in a single layer on the prepared baking sheet. Spread out well and cover with the marinade. Cover with cling film and leave in the fridge to marinate for as long as possible – a minimum of 30 minutes.

Preheat the oven to 220°c/200°c Fan/Gas 7.

Roast the marinated chicken in the oven for 30–35 minutes, until golden and cooked through. Transfer to a warmed dish and sprinkle with coriander, if using, to serve.

VARIATION
If you would like to make a sauce from the leftover cooking juices, pour off the juices into a bowl or jug and skim the fat from the surface and discard. Pour what remains into a saucepan and add 300ml (10fl oz) hot chicken stock. In a small bowl, mix 1 teaspoon of cornflour with 1 tablespoon of cold water to a smooth paste. Add to the pan and mix well. Bring to the boil and heat until thickened. Season to taste and pour over the chicken.

COOK'S NOTES
· Use any cut of chicken you wish. Chicken breasts will cook for 30 minutes, too, though the joints on the bone give the best flavour for this dish.
· Lining the baking sheet with paper makes washing up afterwards much easier.

PREPARE AHEAD
Can be marinated in the fridge for up to 12 hours ahead. Once cooked, the chicken keeps well for up to 48 hours in the fridge.

FREEZE
The marinated raw chicken freezes well.

Burgundy Chicken

A hearty stew that's great for a chilly evening. Best served with mashed potatoes and a green vegetable.

SERVES 6 · PREP TIME: *10 minutes* · COOK TIME: *50 minutes*

750ml (1¼ pints) red
   Burgundy wine
2 tbsp olive oil
8 skinless and boneless
   chicken thighs (see note)
6 rashers of unsmoked
   streaky bacon, chopped
2 red onions, sliced
3 garlic cloves, crushed
45g (1½oz) plain flour
300ml (10fl oz) cold chicken
   stock
leaves from 1 large sprig of
   rosemary, chopped
1 tbsp light muscovado sugar
2 bay leaves
400g (14oz) button
   mushrooms, halved

Preheat the oven to 150°c / 130°c Fan / Gas 2.

Pour the wine into a shallow saucepan and place over a high heat. Bring to a rolling boil and cook for a few minutes to reduce by half.

Heat the oil in a large ovenproof frying pan with a lid, or a cast-iron casserole dish, add the chicken thighs and fry over a high heat for 5–6 minutes on each side, until golden brown all over (see note). Remove from the pan and set aside. Add the bacon and onions to the pan and fry for about 5 minutes, stirring occasionally, then add the garlic and fry for another 30 seconds.

Put the flour in a bowl and add the cold stock gradually, whisking well until smooth. Add the reduced wine to the pan, followed by the flour-thickened stock. Stir over a high heat to deglaze the base of the pan and until the sauce is boiling and has thickened. Return the chicken to the pan, then stir in the rosemary, sugar and bay leaves and season with salt and pepper.

Bring back up to the boil, then cover with the lid and transfer to the oven to cook for about 20 minutes. Remove from the oven, stir in the mushrooms and replace the lid. Return to the oven for a further 10 minutes until the chicken is just cooked. Serve hot.

COOK'S NOTES
· Boneless chicken thighs cook more quickly than thighs on the bone.
· It's important to brown the chicken well, as this will reduce the amount of cooking time needed in the oven later, as well as adding lots of lovely flavour to the dish.

PREPARE AHEAD
Can be made up to a day ahead and reheated. Keeps well in the fridge for up to 3 days.

FREEZE
The cooked dish freezes well.

Piquant Chicken with Tomato and Peppers

Guaranteed to become a family favourite – if you prefer, you could roast the red peppers yourself rather than using peppers from a jar (see page 281).

SERVES 6 · PREP TIME: *10 minutes* · COOK TIME: *15–20 minutes*

5 skinless and boneless chicken breasts, sliced on the diagonal into thin strips
1 tbsp runny honey
2 tbsp olive oil
1 onion, thickly sliced
2 garlic cloves, crushed
1 × 400g jar of roasted red peppers in oil, drained and cut into wide long strips

FOR THE SAUCE
2 × 400g tins of chopped tomatoes
2 tbsp Worcestershire sauce
1½ tbsp grainy mustard
1 tbsp soy sauce
2 tbsp tomato ketchup
2 tbsp tomato purée
1 tbsp runny honey

Season the chicken strips with salt and pepper and toss them in the honey to coat.

Heat a frying pan over a high heat until hot, add the oil and fry the chicken strips for 8–10 minutes until golden all over and cooked through (see note). Remove the chicken with a slotted spoon and set aside on a plate.

Add the onion to the pan, lower the heat to medium–high and fry for 2–3 minutes to soften, then add the garlic and fry for 30 seconds.

Meanwhile, measure all the sauce ingredients into a large bowl, season and mix well. Pour into the pan with the onion and garlic, then add the red peppers. Return the chicken and juices to the pan, cover with a lid and bring to the boil. Reduce the heat and simmer for about 5 minutes until tender.

Serve hot with mashed potato and a green vegetable.

COOK'S NOTE
You may need to fry the chicken in two batches, so as not to overcrowd the pan.

PREPARE AHEAD
Can be made up to 6 hours ahead and reheated.

FREEZE
Freezes well.

Speedy Thai Chicken and Vegetable Curry

There's no need for you to order a Thai takeaway – this is ready in 30 minutes and is much fresher and healthier! Full-fat coconut milk can solidify in the tin, so give it a shake to remix before opening.

SERVES 6 · PREP TIME: *10–15 minutes* **· COOK TIME:** *15–20 minutes*

500g (1lb 2oz) skinless and boneless chicken breasts
2 tbsp sunflower oil
6 spring onions, sliced
1 red pepper, deseeded and diced
150g (5oz) mini courgettes, cut into 1cm (½ in) slices
150g (5oz) button mushrooms, thickly sliced
½–1 fresh red chilli (to taste), deseeded and sliced
2cm (¾in) knob of fresh root ginger, peeled and grated
2 garlic cloves, crushed
1 × 400ml tin of full-fat coconut milk
2–3 tbsp red Thai curry paste
2 tsp soy sauce
2 tsp sweet chilli sauce
1½ tsp cornflour (see note)
juice of ½ lime
handful of coriander leaves, chopped, to garnish

Cut the chicken into strips and season with salt and pepper.

Heat half the oil in a large non-stick frying pan over a high heat. Quickly fry the chicken pieces for 3–4 minutes on each side, until sealed and lightly golden. Remove with a slotted spoon and set aside.

Add the remaining oil to the unwashed pan and reduce the heat to medium. Tip in the spring onions, red pepper, courgettes, mushrooms, chilli, ginger and garlic and fry for 2–3 minutes. Add the coconut milk, Thai curry paste, soy sauce and sweet chilli sauce and bring to the boil, stirring the mixture until smooth.

Return the chicken to the pan with any resting juices, then cover with a lid and simmer for 3–4 minutes, until the chicken is cooked through.

Mix the cornflour with 2½ tablespoons of cold water, then add to the curry with the lime juice. Stir over a low heat until thickened slightly.

Season to taste with salt and pepper. Serve garnished with the coriander, if liked, alongside steamed rice and prawn crackers.

COOK'S NOTES
· Use mini courgettes as they cook more quickly and will stay al dente as they have less of the white middle.
· Traditionally, a Thai sauce is thin; adding a little cornflour at the end thickens it slightly but it will still be fairly loose.

PREPARE AHEAD
Can be made up to 8 hours ahead, then stored in the fridge and reheated to serve.

FREEZE
Not suitable for freezing.

Chicken Escalopes with Crispy Bacon

A weekday supper dish all the family will love, this is also good served with a fried egg. Panko breadcrumbs are a great addition to the store cupboard; they are lighter and crisper than standard breadcrumbs and give a much better texture.

SERVES 6 · PREP TIME: *20 minutes* · COOK TIME: *16–18 minutes per batch*

3 large chicken breasts
1 tbsp grainy mustard
plain flour, for dusting
1 egg, beaten
100g (4oz) panko breadcrumbs
1½ tbsp chopped sage leaves
sunflower oil, for frying
12 rashers of smoked streaky
    bacon (see note)

Slice each breast in half horizontally to give six thin pieces of chicken. Remove the mini fillet if it is still attached (saving it to use later). Sit the breasts on a board, cover with cling film and bash with a meat mallet until about 5mm (¼in) thick (see note).

Season the fillets with salt and pepper and spread one side with a little mustard. Sprinkle the flour on a plate and put the beaten egg in a shallow bowl. Mix the breadcrumbs and sage together on another plate. Dip the chicken in the flour, then the egg and finally coat in the herb breadcrumbs.

Heat a little oil in a large frying pan and fry the bacon over a medium–high heat for 2–3 minutes on each side until crisp. Remove from the pan, drain on kitchen paper and keep hot.

Fry the chicken pieces in the bacon fat in the same hot pan for about 6 minutes on each side, until crisp, golden and cooked through, with no traces of pink. Again, you may need to do this in batches, adding a little more oil each time if necessary. Transfer to a plate lined with kitchen paper to absorb any excess oil, cover with foil and keep warm while you cook the next batch.

Divide the chicken between six plates and place two rashers of crispy bacon on top of each escalope. Serve with a tomato salad.

COOK'S NOTES
· Cooking the chicken in the bacon fat adds to the flavour, so use the best-quality bacon you can.
· If you do not have a meat mallet, use a rolling pin or the base of a saucepan to make the breasts thinner so they cook more quickly.

PREPARE AHEAD
The chicken can be coated up to 6 hours ahead and kept in the fridge.

FREEZE
Not suitable for freezing.

Midweek Chicken, Mozzarella and Tomato Bake

Easy and quick but hearty, this chicken dish will become a firm family favourite. Sun-blushed or sun-soaked tomatoes – only partially dried and usually preserved in oil – have a delicious, concentrated flavour. You can find them in the supermarket in a jar or in a pack in the chiller cabinets.

SERVES 4 · PREP TIME: *20 minutes* · COOK TIME: *25–30 minutes*

400g (14oz) passata
1 tbsp Worcestershire sauce
75g (3oz) full-fat cream cheese
100g (4oz) ready-grated mozzarella cheese (see note)
leaves from 1 small bunch of basil, chopped
6 sun-blushed tomatoes, drained and chopped
4 small skinless and boneless chicken breasts (about 150–175g/5–6oz each)
25g (1oz) Parmesan, grated

You will need a wide-based, shallow ovenproof dish that is large enough to hold all four chicken breasts. Preheat the oven to 200°C/180°C Fan/Gas 6.

Mix the passata with the Worcestershire sauce, season with salt and pepper and pour into the base of the dish.

Mix the cream cheese, mozzarella, basil and tomatoes in a small bowl and season.

Cut a slit three-quarters of the way through each chicken breast to make a pocket. Divide the cheese mixture between the chicken breasts, pushing it into each pocket. Press any remaining mixture on top of the breasts and then season.

Place the chicken in the dish on top of the passata mixture and sprinkle with the Parmesan. Bake in the oven for 25–30 minutes, until the chicken is cooked through, with no traces of pink, and the tomato sauce is bubbling.

Serve with a fresh green salad or steamed green beans.

COOK'S NOTE
Using ready-grated mozzarella from a packet makes this dish extra quick! You could use a ball of buffalo mozzarella instead – you'll just need to tear it into pieces.

PREPARE AHEAD
The dish can be assembled up to 4 hours ahead and kept, covered, in the fridge.

FREEZE
The stuffed chicken breasts can be frozen for up to a month. Defrost thoroughly, then bake in the tomato sauce, sprinkled with Parmesan, to serve.

Chicken and Mushroom Suet Crust Pie

With its easy suet crust and delicious Marsala cream filling, what could be more satisfying than this homemade chicken pie – made from scratch in under an hour? To save time, you could buy all-butter ready-rolled puff pastry and use this instead.

SERVES 6 · PREP TIME: *10 minutes* · COOK TIME: *40–45 minutes*

2 tbsp olive oil

250g (9oz) chestnut mushrooms, sliced

4 skinless and boneless chicken breasts, sliced into thick pieces

1 large onion, roughly chopped

1 garlic clove, crushed

2 tbsp plain flour

150ml (5fl oz) Marsala

200g (7oz) full-fat crème fraîche

2 tbsp chopped parsley

FOR THE PASTRY

100g (4oz) self-raising flour, plus extra for dusting

50g (2oz) suet

¼ tsp salt

1 egg, beaten

You will need a 26cm (10½in) pie dish that can hold about 1.2 litres (2 pints). Preheat the oven to 220°C / 200°C Fan / Gas 7.

Heat half the oil in a large frying pan. Add the mushrooms, season with salt and pepper and fry over a high heat for 3–4 minutes until golden and any liquid has evaporated. Remove from the pan and set aside.

Heat the remaining oil, season the chicken and fry over a high heat for 1–2 minutes on each side until browned – you may need to do this in batches. Remove from the heat and set aside.

Add the onion to the pan, cover with a lid and sweat over a medium heat for 5 minutes until soft. Remove the lid, add the garlic and fry for 30 seconds. Whisk the flour and Marsala in a bowl until smooth then tip into the pan. Add the crème fraîche and stir until thickened and combined. Add the chicken pieces, mushrooms and any resting juices and simmer for a few minutes. Add the parsley, season, then spoon into the pie dish. Set aside to cool.

Meanwhile, to make the pastry, measure the flour, suet and salt into a large bowl and pour in enough water (about 75ml / 2½fl oz) to make a soft dough. Bring together with your hands and lightly knead. Roll out on a floured work surface to about 1cm (½in) thick and large enough to cover the top of the pie dish.

Brush the edge of the dish with a little of the beaten egg, then carefully lay the pastry over the filling. Trim the edges and press to seal. Brush with more beaten egg and make a small hole in the middle of the pastry to allow steam to escape. Place on a baking sheet and bake in the oven for 25–30 minutes until well risen and lightly golden.

Serve with new potatoes and a green vegetable.

PREPARE AHEAD
The pie can be assembled up to 6 hours ahead and baked to serve.

FREEZE
The pre-baked pie freezes well. Bake straight from frozen for 40–45 minutes.

Roast Venison with Peppercorn Sauce

Venison treated like fillet of beef – tender, succulent and indulgent. The timing here is for rare, which is the best way to serve venison, but you can cook it longer if you prefer. Roast for 14–15 minutes for medium and 18–20 minutes for well done.

SERVES 4–6 · PREP TIME: *15 minutes, plus marinating* **· COOK TIME:** *20 minutes, plus resting*

500g (1lb 2oz) boneless
    middle-cut venison fillet
3 tbsp olive oil
1 tsp chopped thyme leaves
1 tbsp coarsely ground or
    crushed black peppercorns

FOR THE PEPPERCORN SAUCE
a knob of butter
1 garlic clove, crushed
2 tbsp brandy
300ml (10fl oz) double cream
2 tbsp chopped parsley leaves
2 tsp coarsely ground or
    crushed black peppercorns

Preheat the oven 220°c / 200°c Fan / Gas 7.

Trim any membrane from the venison, then rub the oil, thyme and a little of the pepper into the meat. Rub in well and then leave to marinate if time allows.

Heat a dry frying pan until hot. Lightly roll the venison in the ground / crushed peppercorns and sear in the hot pan for a couple of minutes on each side so that it is golden brown all over, then transfer to a small roasting tin.

Roast the venison in the oven for 12 minutes (a little less if you have just browned it and it has not yet cooled down). Leave to rest out of the oven, covered in foil, for about 10 minutes (see note).

To make the sauce, melt the butter in a pan over a medium heat, add the garlic and fry for 2 minutes. Pour in the brandy and boil for 10 seconds. Add the double cream, bring back up to the boil, stirring, then season with salt. Add the parsley, ground / crushed peppercorns and any resting juices from the roasting tin.

Carve the venison and serve with the peppercorn sauce.

COOK'S NOTES
· The resting time is key to ensuring the meat is perfectly cooked.
· You could add a little lemon juice to cut through the richness, if you liked.

PREPARE AHEAD
The venison can be browned up to 12 hours ahead, then roasted to serve. The sauce can be made up to a day ahead and kept in the fridge; gently reheat and add the parsley just before serving.

FREEZE
Not suitable for freezing.

Pork, Lamb and Beef

Italian Galette

A quick and easy way to make a savoury tart. Using shop-bought puff pastry is a joy – be sure to buy the all-butter variety as this is the real deal with the best flavour. Serve the galette with a large salad or slaw.

SERVES 4 · PREP TIME: *15 minutes, plus chilling* · COOK TIME: *20–25 minutes*

plain flour, for dusting
1 × 320g packet of ready-rolled all-butter puff pastry
1 egg, beaten
2 tbsp sun-dried tomato paste
1 x 200g goat's cheese log, cut into thin slices
6 slices of Parma ham
200g (7oz) cherry tomatoes, halved
25g (1oz) pitted green olives
1 tsp thyme leaves

TO SERVE
rocket leaves
a few Parmesan shavings (optional)
olive oil and balsamic glaze, for drizzling

Preheat the oven to 220°C/200°C Fan/Gas 7 and line a large baking sheet with baking paper.

Scatter a little flour on your worktop, sit the puff pastry on top and re-roll into a circle about 28cm (11in) in diameter. Crimp the edges to give a twisted, rope-like effect, then brush the edges with beaten egg. Transfer to the prepared baking sheet and place in the fridge to chill for 10 minutes, if time allows.

Prick the base of the pastry all over with a fork, then use the back of a spoon to spread with the sun-dried tomato paste. Arrange the goat's cheese slices on top and season with a little salt and pepper (see note), then scatter over the tomatoes, olives and thyme leaves.

Bake on the top shelf of the oven for 15 minutes.

Remove from the oven, scrunch up each slice of ham and arrange on top of the galette. Return to the oven to cook for another 5–10 minutes or until the ham is crispy and the pastry is golden underneath (see note).

Scatter with rocket leaves and Parmesan shavings, if you like, and drizzle over a little olive oil and balsamic glaze to serve.

COOK'S NOTES
· Be careful not to over-season with salt as the olives and Parma ham can be quite salty.
· To check the pastry base is cooked right to the centre, lift an edge carefully with a palette knife to see that it is evenly golden underneath.

PREPARE AHEAD
The galette can be assembled 2–3 hours before baking and kept in the fridge.

FREEZE
Not suitable for freezing.

Marinated Mango Pork Medallions

Slices of pork fillet with a quick, tasty sauce. These would work well on a barbecue too. Serve with sweet potato wedges and a crunchy coleslaw.

SERVES 4 · PREP TIME: *5 minutes, plus marinating* · COOK TIME: *5–10 minutes, plus resting*

2 tbsp mango chutney
2 tbsp soy sauce
1 tbsp grated fresh root ginger
350g (12oz) thick pork fillet, trimmed and cut into slices 1cm (½in) thick
1 tbsp sunflower oil

Mix the mango chutney, soy sauce and ginger together in a large bowl. Add the sliced pork fillet and coat in the marinade, then set aside for 10 minutes at room temperature.

Heat a large, wide frying pan over a high heat until hot (see note) and add the oil. Season the pork with salt and pepper and add to the pan. Fry for about 2 minutes on each side until golden and just cooked through. You may need to do this in batches so as not to overcrowd the pan. Transfer the pork to a plate and leave to rest, covered with foil, for 5 minutes.

While the pork is resting, pour any remaining marinade from the bowl into the pan, then deglaze with a splash of hot water and stir to make a dark, gingery jus.

Divide the pork between four plates and spoon over the jus to serve.

COOK'S NOTE
Frying over a high heat in a wide-based, non-stick pan is the quickest way to cook the pork.

PREPARE AHEAD
The pork can be marinated in the fridge up to a day in advance.

FREEZE
The marinated raw pork can be frozen for up to a month.

Marinated Roast Fillet of Pork with Mustard and Sage Sauce

This delicious pork roast is on the table in under an hour, making it an easy Sunday lunch or dinner with friends – faster than a traditional roast too. Two types of mustard are included here: do use Dijon in the marinade and not a grainy variety, as mustard seeds would scorch when roasted. And use a sturdy roasting tin as it will be put on the hob to make the sauce: a good, thick-grade metal pan won't buckle on the direct heat.

SERVES 4 · PREP TIME: *10 minutes, plus marinating* · COOK TIME: *30–35 minutes*

1 large pork fillet (about 350g/12oz)
1½ tbsp chopped sage
1½ tbsp chopped thyme leaves

FOR THE MARINADE
1 tbsp Dijon mustard
2 tsp maple syrup
1 tbsp olive oil
1 garlic clove, crushed

FOR THE MUSTARD SAUCE
100ml (3½fl oz) white wine
150ml (5fl oz) double cream
2 tsp grainy mustard
½ tsp cornflour (optional)
1 tsp chopped sage

Preheat the oven to 220°c/200°c Fan/Gas 7.

Trim any excess membrane from the pork and place the meat in a shallow dish. Mix all of the marinade ingredients together. Add the marinade to the pork and massage it into the meat. Leave in the fridge for 10 minutes to marinate.

Scatter the chopped herbs over a large chopping board, then roll the marinated pork in the herbs to coat the meat. Season with salt and pepper and place in a small roasting tin, scooping up any leftover marinade to add to the pork. Roast in the oven for 20–25 minutes until firm to touch and just cooked.

Remove from the tin and leave to rest on a plate for 5 minutes, covered with foil, while you make the sauce.

Pour the wine into the warm roasting tin. Place on the hob over a high heat and bring to the boil, stirring to release all the sticky residue. Boil to reduce by a third, then add the cream and mustard and whisk to mix well. Slake the cornflour, if using, in 1 tablespoon of water (see note). Add to the sauce to thicken, stirring as it cooks for 2–3 minutes. Season well and stir in the sage and any juices from the rested pork.

Slice the pork and serve with mash, green vegetables and the mustard and sage sauce.

COOK'S NOTES
- Use fresh herbs only; dried herbs won't have the same depth of flavour.
- You may not need an extra thickener, so do leave out the cornflour if the addition of double cream already makes it a good pouring consistency.

PREPARE AHEAD
Can be marinated in the fridge up to a day ahead.

FREEZE
The raw, marinated meat freezes well for up to a month.

Rack of Lamb with Bulgur Wheat Salad and Spiced Yoghurt Sauce

Cooked in the oven or on the barbecue and served with a flavoursome salad and a spicy yoghurt sauce, this is a lovely way to serve a rack of lamb on a spring evening. Use couscous instead of bulgur wheat, if preferred.

SERVES 4 · PREP TIME: *15 minutes, plus marinating* · COOK TIME: *15 minutes, plus resting*

2 small trimmed racks of lamb
2 garlic cloves, bashed
leaves from 2 sprigs of
    rosemary, roughly chopped
2 tbsp olive oil
250g (9oz) bulgur wheat
500ml (18fl oz) hot vegetable
    stock
1 bunch of spring onions, sliced
½ fresh red chilli, deseeded
    and diced
leaves from 1 large bunch
    of mint, chopped

FOR THE DRESSING
juice and finely grated zest
    of 1 large lemon
1 tbsp white wine vinegar
6 tbsp olive oil
1 garlic clove, crushed

FOR THE YOGHURT SAUCE
200g (7oz) Greek-style natural
    yoghurt
leaves from 1 bunch of mint,
    chopped
juice of ½ lemon
½–1 tsp harissa paste (to taste)

Preheat the oven to 200°c / 180°c Fan / Gas 6.

Put the lamb in a freezer bag with the garlic, rosemary and olive oil. Season with salt and pepper and massage the flavourings into the lamb, then leave to marinate for 5–10 minutes.

Heat a large frying pan until hot. Add the lamb and fry over a high heat for 2–3 minutes until browned all over. Place on a baking sheet and roast in the oven for about 10 minutes until golden (see note).

Remove from the oven and leave to rest on a warm plate, covered with foil, for 5 minutes.

Meanwhile, put the bulgur wheat in a medium saucepan, pour in the stock, cover with a lid and bring to the boil. Boil for 1 minute, then remove from the heat and leave to stand for 10 minutes until all of the liquid has been absorbed. Spoon the bulgur wheat into a large bowl and add the spring onions, chilli and mint.

Mix all of the dressing ingredients together and pour over the bulgur wheat salad. Season well with salt and pepper.

Mix all of the sauce ingredients together in a bowl and season well.

Carve the lamb between the bones and serve 3 or 4 chops per person, along with the bulgur wheat salad and yoghurt sauce.

COOK'S NOTE

This is the quickest of roast lamb dishes. Racks of lamb vary in size, so you may find yours takes only 8 minutes to roast, or it may need longer.

PREPARE AHEAD

The bulgur wheat salad and the yoghurt sauce can be made up to a day ahead and kept in the fridge.

FREEZE

Not suitable for freezing.

Minted Lamb Meatballs with Yoghurt Dip

This is one of my favourite ways to serve minced lamb. Use shop-bought mint sauce from a jar, unless you have an abundance of fresh mint in the garden for making your own. The sauce gives a lovely intense flavour and is something I always have to hand in the cupboard.

MAKES 30 · **PREP TIME:** *15 minutes* · **COOK TIME:** *8–10 minutes*

2 slices bread
500g (1lb 2oz) lean minced
    lamb
1 tbsp mint sauce
1 garlic clove, crushed
6 spring onions, chopped
2 tbsp sunflower oil

FOR THE YOGHURT DIP

2 spring onions, finely
    chopped
½ garlic clove, crushed
200g (7oz) natural yoghurt
2 tsp mint sauce
1 tbsp chopped mint leaves
juice of ½ lemon
1 tbsp chopped parsley

Place the bread in a food processor and whizz until crumbs. Add the lamb, mint sauce, garlic and spring onions, season with salt and pepper, and whizz until the mixture comes together and is finely chopped. Remove from the processor and shape into 30 even-sized balls, each about the size of a walnut.

Place all the ingredients for the yoghurt dip in a small bowl, season and mix until combined. Spoon into a pretty bowl to serve.

Pour the oil into a large frying pan over a medium–high heat, add the meatballs and fry for 8–10 minutes, turning continuously (see note), until golden brown all over and cooked through. Drain on kitchen paper. You may need to cook the meatballs in two batches so there is plenty of room in the frying pan to turn them.

Arrange the hot meatballs on a serving plate and serve with the dip, flatbreads (such as the Garlic Herb Flatbreads on page 38) and a tomato salad.

COOK'S NOTE
Use two forks to turn the meatballs easily as you cook them.

PREPARE AHEAD
The meatballs can made up to a day in advance and cooked to serve. The dip can be prepared up to 2 days ahead and stored in the fridge; the flavour will intensify the longer it is kept.

FREEZE
The uncooked meatballs freeze well.

Lamb Tagine

For the TV series accompanying this book, I travelled to Morocco where tagines, like this, are a staple dish. They may be slow to cook but they are quick to make. This is my quick version as some tagines take three hours to cook. The spices used here are a classic combination for tagine recipes and give a wonderful depth of flavour. All these spices are good to keep in your store cupboard, so you always have them to hand.

SERVES 6 · PREP TIME: *30 minutes* · COOK TIME: *1 hour 40 minutes–2 hours 10 minutes*

2–3 tbsp sunflower oil

750g (1lb 10oz) lamb neck fillet, sliced into 2–3cm (¾–1¼in) pieces

2 large onions, sliced

3 celery sticks, sliced

2 garlic cloves, crushed

4cm (1½in) knob of fresh root ginger, peeled and grated (see note on page 114)

1 tbsp ground cumin

1 tbsp ground coriander

2 tsp ground cinnamon

1 × 400g tin of chopped tomatoes

450ml (15fl oz) chicken or lamb stock

2 tbsp tomato purée

2 tsp harissa paste

1 tbsp runny honey

8 ready-to-eat dried apricots, quartered

2 preserved lemons, sliced into 8 pieces and any pips removed (see note)

1 × 400g tin of chickpeas, drained and rinsed

2 tbsp chopped parsley

Preheat the oven to 150°c/130°c Fan/Gas 2.

Heat a deep ovenproof frying pan with a lid, or a large cast-iron casserole dish, over a high heat. Add the oil and the lamb and fry for 3–4 minutes or until the meat is golden brown all over. You may need to do this in two batches. Use a slotted spoon to transfer the meat to a plate.

Add the onions and celery to the pan and fry over a medium heat for 3–4 minutes until starting to soften but not browned. Add the garlic and ginger, then sprinkle in the spices and stir to coat the vegetables. Cook for 10 seconds, add the tomatoes, stock, tomato purée, harissa paste, honey, apricots and preserved lemons. Bring to the boil, stirring, and then return the lamb and any juices to the pan. Season with salt and pepper, cover with the lid and transfer to the oven to cook for 1 hour.

Remove from the oven, stir in the chickpeas and check the seasoning, then return to the oven, uncovered, and cook for another ½–1 hour or until the onions have softened and the meat is tender (see note).

Sprinkle with the chopped parsley and serve with the Nutty Wholemeal Couscous Salad or Moroccan Summer Salad (see pages 81 and 78).

COOK'S NOTES

· Preserved lemons are available to buy in the
specialist ingredient section of good supermarkets.
They have been preserved in salt so the skin softens
and can be eaten.

· The cooking time depends on the size of the lamb
pieces – smaller chunks may take a bit less time
to cook.

PREPARE AHEAD

Can be made up to a day ahead and reheated.

FREEZE

The cooked dish freezes well.

Marinated Rosemary Lamb Steaks with Red Peppers

Lamb steaks can often be forgotten in favour of the large joints. Cooked in the right way, they are tender and full of flavour, and quick to prepare as well.

SERVES 4 · PREP TIME: *15 minutes* · COOK TIME: *20–25 minutes, plus resting*

4 × 150g (5oz) lean lamb steaks (from the leg)
2 red peppers, quartered and deseeded
4 banana shallots, peeled, trimmed and sliced in half lengthways through the root
1 tbsp olive oil
1 tbsp balsamic glaze

FOR THE MARINADE
2 tbsp chopped rosemary leaves
2 tbsp olive oil
1 garlic clove, crushed
juice of ½ small lemon

Preheat the grill to high.

Mix the marinade ingredients together in a bowl. Add the lamb and set aside to marinate for 10 minutes, or longer if possible.

Meanwhile, sit the peppers, cut side down, on one side of the grill pan. Toss the shallots in the oil and season with salt and pepper. Arrange them on the other side. Slide under the grill to cook for 10–12 minutes, turning the shallots halfway through the cooking time, until the pepper skins are blackened and the shallots golden and slightly charred. Immediately transfer the peppers to a bowl, cover with cling film, and leave to sweat for 10 minutes to loosen the skins.

Meanwhile, heat a griddle or heavy-based frying pan over a high heat until hot. Remove the steaks from the marinade and quickly sear on both sides. Reduce the heat and fry for 3–5 minutes on each side until golden brown but still slightly pink in the middle. Transfer to a plate, cover with foil and leave to rest for 5 minutes.

While the lamb is resting, peel and discard the skins of the grilled peppers then cut the flesh into large pieces. Add to the pan with the shallots to heat through.

Arrange the vegetables on a plate. Cut the lamb into slices and place on top. Mix the balsamic glaze with 4 tablespoons of water and add to the pan with any remaining marinade and resting juices. Deglaze the pan for 30 seconds and pour the sauce over the lamb to serve.

COOK'S NOTES
- If you prefer to make this dish on the hob only, chargrill the peppers in a griddle pan over a high heat. Alternatively, use a jar of roasted red peppers and simply heat in the pan with the shallots.
- Serving your lamb pink not only keeps down the cooking time but means the meat will be beautifully tender. The cooking time will also depend on how thick your steaks are.

PREPARE AHEAD
The peppers and shallots can be cooked up to 3 hours ahead and reheated to serve. The lamb can be marinated overnight and kept in the fridge.

FREEZE
The cooked dish is not suitable for freezing. The lamb steaks could be frozen raw in the marinade, ready to cook.

Quick Beef Ragù

Mince is a speedy way to feed the family and economical too. My ragù includes lots of fresh vegetables and is good to serve with pasta, rice or in a bake. Reducing the wine is the secret to locking in the flavour, along with cutting the vegetables into small pieces (see note). Have everything prepared and ready to go and you can make this ragù in around 30 minutes.

SERVES 6 · PREP TIME: *15 minutes* · COOK TIME: *30–40 minutes*

500ml (18fl oz) red wine
1 tbsp oil
2 celery sticks, finely diced
1 small leek, finely chopped
1 large onion, finely chopped
1 large carrot, finely diced
2 garlic cloves, crushed
500g (1lb 2oz) lean minced beef
2 tbsp plain flour
500g (1lb 2oz) passata
1 tbsp sun-dried tomato paste (see note)
2 tsp chopped marjoram leaves, plus extra to garnish
2 tsp chopped rosemary leaves
2 bay leaves
1 tsp light muscovado sugar
grated Parmesan, to serve

Preheat the oven to 180°C/160°C Fan/Gas 4.

Pour the wine into a wide-based saucepan and bring to the boil. Continue to boil for 5–10 minutes until reduced by a third.

Meanwhile, heat the oil in a large ovenproof pan with a lid. Add the vegetables and fry over a medium–high heat for 6–7 minutes until beginning to soften. Add the garlic and fry for 10 seconds, then tip in the minced beef and brown all over for 3–4 minutes, breaking it up into smaller pieces with a spatula as it fries.

Sprinkle in the flour and stir over the heat for 2–3 minutes. Add the reduced wine with the passata, tomato paste, herbs and sugar, and season with salt and pepper. Bring to the boil, cover with the lid and transfer to the oven, or keep on the hob over a gentle heat, to cook for 20–25 minutes until just tender.

Check the seasoning, remove the bay leaves and serve piping hot with pasta or rice, sprinkled with chopped marjoram and grated Parmesan.

COOK'S NOTES
· Cut the vegetables into tiny pieces – each about the size of a raisin – to help them cook quickly.
· You can use standard tomato paste, but the sun-dried variety adds extra flavour and is readily available in jars or tubes.

PREPARE AHEAD
Can be made up to 2 days ahead, kept in the fridge and reheated.

FREEZE
Freeze for up to a month.

Thai Green Beef Curry

I have used green Thai curry paste for this dish, but you could swap for red, if you prefer. This could be combined with the Korma-style Chicken Curry and the Cauliflower, Aubergine and Lemon Grass Curry (see page 221) as a feast for friends.

SERVES 6 • PREP TIME: *15 minutes, plus marinating* • COOK TIME: *15 minutes*

2 × 250g (9oz) rump or sirloin steaks
2 tbsp sweet chilli sauce
2 tbsp sunflower oil
1 onion, thinly sliced
1 red pepper, deseeded and thinly sliced
3cm (1¼in) knob of fresh root ginger, peeled and finely diced (see note on page 114)
2 × 400ml tins of full-fat coconut milk
1 lemon grass stalk, bashed
3 tbsp green Thai curry paste
2 tsp light muscovado sugar
2 tsp fish sauce
1 × 225g tin of bamboo shoots, drained
juice of ½ lime (or to taste)
2 tbsp chopped Thai basil leaves (see note)

Sit the steaks on a board and trim off any fat, then cover with cling film and bash with a meat mallet or rolling pin until half the thickness. Cut into thin strips and tip into a bowl, then season with salt and pepper and pour over the sweet chilli sauce. Toss together and set aside to marinate for 10 minutes.

Heat the oil in a deep pan and quickly fry the marinated strips of beef over a high heat for 2–3 minutes until browned but still pink inside, then set aside. Cook in batches if necessary; you want the beef to sear quickly but not stew in its juices (see note).

Add the onion, red pepper and ginger to the pan and fry over a high heat for 5 minutes. Pour in the coconut milk and add the lemon grass, green Thai paste, sugar, fish sauce and bamboo shoots. Bring to the boil, then cover with the lid, reduce the heat and simmer for about 5 minutes. Return the beef to the pan and quickly bring back up to the boil to heat it through. Check the seasoning, then remove the lemon grass and discard, and add the lime juice.

Scatter with the basil leaves and serve with rice, or rice noodles, and prawn crackers.

COOK'S NOTES
· Thai basil leaves have a lovely aniseed flavour, but if it is not available, you could use fresh basil instead.
· Do not overcook the beef; it should be pink and tender.

PREPARE AHEAD
Can be made up to 4 hours ahead and reheated gently, adding the basil to serve.

FREEZE
Not suitable for freezing.

Beef Fillet with Creamy Stilton and Mushroom Sauce

This is a special supper dish using beef fillet – the finest, most tender cut. The tail end of the fillet is more reasonably priced than the centre cut. You can use a less expensive cut, such as rump or ribeye, if you prefer, but be sure not to overcook it!

SERVES 4–6 · PREP TIME: *15 minutes* · COOK TIME: *12 minutes*

2 tbsp sunflower oil

300g (11oz) beef tail fillet, sliced into very thin strips

1 onion, finely chopped

250g (9oz) chestnut mushrooms, sliced

200g (7oz) wild mushrooms (such as oyster or shiitake), halved

2 garlic cloves, crushed

1 bunch of spring onions, sliced

3 tbsp brandy

150ml (5fl oz) double cream

1 tbsp grainy mustard

50g (2oz) Stilton or other blue cheese, grated

juice of ½ lemon

1 bunch of chives, snipped

Heat half the oil in a deep frying pan. Season the beef with salt and pepper and fry over a high heat for a couple of minutes until just sealed and lightly browned (see note). Use a slotted spoon to transfer to a plate.

Heat the remaining oil in the pan. Add the onion and fry over a high heat for 3–4 minutes, stirring until starting to soften. Add the mushrooms, then cover with a lid, reduce the heat and cook for 3 minutes or until the liquid has come out of the mushrooms. Remove the lid, add the garlic and spring onions and fry over a high heat for another 3 minutes or until the mushrooms have browned. Add the brandy, cream, mustard and Stilton, stirring until the cheese has melted, then bring to the boil, season and return the beef to the pan. Heat through for a minute until piping hot.

Remove from the heat and stir in the lemon juice and half the chives. Check the seasoning and serve with mashed potatoes or rice and sprinkled with the remaining chives.

COOK'S NOTE
Make sure the beef slices are still pink when you transfer them to the dish; they need only a minute or two to sear all over.

PREPARE AHEAD
Best made and served immediately.

FREEZE
Not suitable for freezing.

Rice, Noodles and Pasta

Mushroom and Asparagus Risotto

My quick risotto is full of flavour from all the fresh ingredients. An oven-baked risotto is a good alternative – prepare as here, but add all the stock at once and pop into the oven, preheated to 200°C/180°C Fan/Gas 6, to cook for around 20 minutes. Stir in the mushrooms and asparagus tips 3 minutes before the end, then finish off with the cheese, butter and chives before serving.

SERVES 4 · PREP TIME: *15 minutes* · COOK TIME: *30 minutes*

1 tbsp oil
1 large onion, chopped
1 large garlic clove, crushed
275g (10oz) risotto rice
100ml (3½fl oz) white wine
150g (5oz) asparagus spears,
    stalks sliced into rounds
    and tips reserved
about 800ml (1 pint 7fl oz) hot
    chicken or vegetable stock
350g (12oz) mixed button and
    chestnut mushrooms,
    sliced
75g (3oz) Parmesan, grated
1 bunch of chives, snipped
a large knob of butter

Heat the oil in a wide-based shallow saucepan (see note). Add the onions and garlic and fry for a few minutes over a high heat. Add the rice and stir in the mixture to coat the grains. Pour in the wine and boil for a few minutes until nearly evaporated. Toss in the sliced asparagus stalks and add the hot stock, a ladleful at a time, stirring over the high heat, until all the stock has been absorbed, and the rice is just tender. Make sure that each spoonful of stock is absorbed before adding the next. From when the first ladle of stock is added, it should take around 20 minutes to cook.

Add the mushrooms and the asparagus tips and stir for about 3 minutes until well combined with the rice and just softened.

Remove from the heat. Add the Parmesan, chives and butter and season to taste with salt and pepper. Stir and cover with a lid, then leave to stand for 2 minutes before serving.

COOK'S NOTE
Use a wide-based pan so the liquid evaporates quickly.

PREPARE AHEAD
Best made and served immediately, though any leftovers can be quickly chilled and made into risotto cakes to fry and enjoy the following day.

FREEZE
Not suitable for freezing.

Crayfish and Prawn Nasi Goreng

Nasi Goreng, or Indonesian fried rice, has long been a favourite dish of mine. It's usually made with strips of golden chicken, but I have replaced these with prawns and crayfish tails (see note) for a different take on the classic recipe. To make the dish even more authentic, you could serve it with a fried egg on top of each portion.

SERVES 4–6 • PREP TIME: *15 minutes* • COOK TIME: *15–20 minutes*

275g (10oz) long-grain rice
3 tbsp sunflower oil
2 red onions, finely chopped
6 rashers of smoked streaky bacon, chopped
1 red pepper, deseeded and thinly sliced
2 large garlic cloves, crushed
200g (7oz) button mushrooms, sliced
1½ tsp medium curry powder
4 tbsp soy sauce
1 tbsp sweet chilli sauce
juice of ½ lemon
120g (4½oz) peeled, cooked crayfish tails
150g (5oz) small, peeled, cooked prawns
1 tbsp chopped parsley, to serve

Cook the rice in a pan of boiling water according to the packet instructions, then drain and leave in the colander to dry out a little.

Meanwhile, heat the oil in a large frying pan over a high heat. Add the onions and bacon and fry for 3–4 minutes until the bacon is crisp. Add the red pepper, garlic and mushrooms and fry for another 2 minutes. Stir in the curry powder and soy sauce.

Tip in the cooked rice and fry for 2–3 minutes, still over a high heat, and stir well to combine all the ingredients.

Add the sweet chilli sauce, lemon juice and seafood. Season with salt and pepper and toss until everything is combined and piping hot.

Scatter with the parsley before serving.

COOK'S NOTE
Using cooked prawns and crayfish tails makes this dish super-speedy.

PREPARE AHEAD
Can be made up to 3 hours ahead and placed in an ovenproof dish. Store in the fridge and reheat in the oven until piping hot before serving.

FREEZE
Not suitable for freezing.

Romano Pepper and Herb Penne

Crispy Parma ham, red peppers and fresh herbs is such a lovely flavour combination. Parma ham usually comes in packets of six to seven slices – use the whole packet. Swap the ham for thin rashers of streaky bacon, if you prefer.

SERVES 4 • **PREP TIME:** *10 minutes* • **COOK TIME:** *10–15 minutes*

275g (10oz) penne pasta

6–7 slices Parma ham, snipped into small pieces

1 tbsp olive oil

4 spring onions, chopped (see note)

150g (5oz) roasted red peppers in oil (from a jar), drained and chopped (see note)

1 large garlic clove, crushed

200g (7oz) full-fat crème fraîche

1 × 30g packet of flat-leaf parsley, leaves roughly chopped

1 × 30g packet of basil, leaves roughly chopped

30g (10z) Parmesan, finely grated

Cook the pasta in boiling salted water according to the packet instructions, then drain, reserving some of the cooking water.

Meanwhile, place a large frying pan over a high heat. Fry the Parma ham for a few minutes, stirring occasionally, until crispy. Remove with a slotted spoon and set aside.

Add the oil to the pan, along with the spring onions, peppers and garlic and fry, stirring occasionally, for 2 minutes.

Add the crème fraîche and bring to the boil, then add the drained pasta with half the crispy ham, most of the herbs and some salt and pepper. Toss over the heat for a few minutes.

Add the cheese and a splash of the reserved cooking water if the sauce seems too thick, and sprinkle over the remaining crispy ham and herbs to serve.

COOK'S NOTES
- Try using kitchen scissors to cut the spring onions quickly.
- Using chargrilled skinned peppers in oil from a jar makes this dish very quick – they are an excellent time saver. You can roast and skin your own peppers of course, if you prefer (see page 281).

PREPARE AHEAD
The ham can be pan-fried up to 3 hours ahead.

FREEZE
Not suitable for freezing.

Spaghetti alle Vongole

A classic spaghetti dish with clams and a delicious white wine sauce. To purge the clams of sand before cooking, simply place them in a bowl of cold water and leave for 20 minutes. As the clams breathe they filter water so the sand is pushed out.

SERVES 4 • **PREP TIME:** *10 minutes* • **COOK TIME:** *10 minutes*

275g (10oz) spaghetti
4 tbsp olive oil
2 large banana shallots, finely chopped
1 fresh red chilli, deseeded and finely diced
2 garlic cloves, crushed
750g–1kg (1lb 10oz–2lb 4oz) small fresh clams, cleaned
175ml (6fl oz) white wine
juice of ½ lemon
1 large bunch of flat-leaf parsley, chopped

Cook the spaghetti in boiling salted water according to the packet instructions, then drain.

While the pasta is cooking, heat 2 tablespoons of the oil over a high heat in a wide, deep pan with a lid. Add the shallots and chilli to the pan and fry for 2 minutes, stirring, then add the garlic and fry for 10 seconds. Tip in the clams and stir everything together. Pour in the wine and bring to the boil for 2 minutes, then cover with the lid and boil for 2–3 minutes until all the clams have opened (discard any that don't open).

Add the drained pasta to the clams, season well with salt and pepper and toss together. Stir through the lemon juice and parsley and drizzle over the remaining oil.

Serve the clams at once while piping hot, spooning over the cooking liquor at the end. Don't forget to put out extra bowls for the discarded shells.

COOK'S NOTE
If any of the clams are open before cooking, give them a quick tap and discard any that fail to close. You should also discard any clams that remain closed at the end of cooking.

PREPARE AHEAD
Best made and served immediately.

FREEZE
Not suitable for freezing.

Spaghetti with Salmon, Chilli and White Wine

Light and fresh, this is an ideal dish for a summer's evening and always goes down well.

SERVES 4 · PREP TIME: *10 minutes* · COOK TIME: *12–15 minutes*

300g (11oz) spaghetti

150ml (5fl oz) white wine

2 hot-smoked salmon fillets, skinned and sliced into large strips (see note)

4 tbsp olive oil

2 banana shallots, thinly sliced

1 fresh red chilli, deseeded and diced

3 tbsp chopped parsley

1 heaped tbsp chopped tarragon leaves

juice of ½ lemon

freshly grated Parmesan, to serve (optional)

Cook the spaghetti in boiling salted water according to the packet instructions, then drain, reserving some of the cooking water.

Meanwhile, pour the wine into a wide saucepan, cover with a lid and bring to the boil. Add the salmon, cover again with the lid and gently simmer for 3–4 minutes until the fish is just cooked. Remove from the heat and set aside.

Heat 2 tablespoons of the olive oil in a large frying pan. Add the shallots and fry over a medium heat for 5 minutes. Add the chilli and fry for a further 15 seconds.

Remove the salmon from the pan with a slotted spoon and set aside. Pour the wine from the pan into the shallot mixture, then add the drained spaghetti with the salmon, chopped herbs, lemon juice and remaining oil. Season with salt and pepper, add a good splash of the reserved cooking water to loosen the sauce, if needed, and gently toss over the heat for a few minutes (see note).

Serve with some grated Parmesan, if you like.

COOK'S NOTES
· Use standard fresh salmon fillets, if you prefer.
· Be careful not to toss too energetically, as you want to keep the salmon in large pieces.

PREPARE AHEAD
Best served straight away.

FREEZE
Not suitable for freezing.

RICE, NOODLES AND PASTA

Tagliatelle with Mushrooms and Stilton

This is the perfect recipe for using up any tail ends of Stilton or other blue cheese.
The cheese adds depth to the overall flavour without being overpowering.

SERVES 4 · PREP TIME: *10 minutes* · COOK TIME: *10 minutes*

250g (9oz) tagliatelle
6 sun-dried tomatoes in oil
(from a jar), drained and
sliced into strips
350g (12oz) chestnut
mushrooms, sliced
1 garlic clove, crushed
150ml (5fl oz) double cream
100g (4oz) Stilton or other
blue cheese, finely
crumbled
30g (1oz) Parmesan, grated
juice of ½ lemon
4 tbsp chopped parsley

Cook the pasta in boiling salted water according to the packet instructions until just tender (see note), then drain, reserving some of the cooking water.

Meanwhile, measure 2 tablespoons of oil from the sun-dried tomato jar into a large frying pan. Add the mushrooms and fry for a couple of minutes over a high heat until starting to brown, then add the garlic and fry for 30 seconds. Pour in the cream and bring to the boil. Add both cheeses, stirring to melt them, then add the lemon juice and sun-dried tomatoes. Add the drained pasta and some reserved cooking water, if needed to loosen the sauce. Season well with salt and pepper and toss together.

Stir half the parsley through the pasta, and scatter with the remaining parsley before serving.

COOK'S NOTE
You could save valuable minutes by using fresh tagliatelle, which take only 3–4 minutes in boiling water.

PREPARE AHEAD
Make the sauce a couple of hours in advance and reheat before serving. The pasta can be cooked up to an hour ahead and reheated in the hot sauce.

FREEZE
Not suitable for freezing.

Rice Noodle and Vegetable Stir-Fry

Stir-fries like this are all in the preparation – once that is done, it takes no time at all to whip up a fresh, healthy meal that's full of flavour, colour and crunch.

SERVES 4–6 · PREP TIME: *20 minutes* · COOK TIME: *10 minutes*

150g (5oz) fine rice noodles (see note)

2 tbsp sunflower oil

2cm (¾in) knob of fresh root ginger, peeled and finely chopped or grated (see note on page 114)

1 red pepper, deseeded and thinly sliced

1 carrot, thinly sliced into matchsticks (see note)

200g (7oz) pak choi, white and green parts separated and finely shredded

1 tbsp soy sauce

juice of 1 small lemon

1 tsp caster sugar

1 tsp sesame oil

Cook the noodles according to the packet instructions, then drain and refresh under cold water. Drain well once again. Set aside.

Heat the oil in a large frying pan. Add the ginger, red pepper and carrot and fry over a high heat for about 3 minutes. Tip in the white parts of the pak choi and fry for 1 minute. Add the drained noodles, soy sauce, lemon juice, sugar and sesame oil and toss until heated through and well combined. Use two spatulas to help to toss everything together. Season with salt and pepper and finally add the green parts of the pak choi, tossing until just wilted.

Serve in a large, warmed bowl.

COOK'S NOTES
· Rice noodles are clear, but yellow egg noodles would work well in this dish, too.
· For speed, save on chopping and coarsely grate the carrots, then add them with the pak choi stems.

PREPARE AHEAD
Best made and served at once.

FREEZE
Not suitable for freezing.

Asian Beef and Red Pepper Stir-Fry

A dish with a Chinese influence. Bashing the steak first tenderises it and pan-frying it as a piece rather than in strips gives a more succulent flavour.

SERVES 4 · PREP TIME: *20 minutes* · **COOK TIME:** *15 minutes*

2 × 200g (7oz) rump steaks, trimmed (see note)
150g (5oz) fine egg noodles (about 2 nests)
3 tbsp sunflower oil
2 red peppers, deseeded and thinly sliced
1 onion, thinly sliced
½ head of Chinese leaves, white and green parts separated and very finely sliced
1 bunch of coriander, chopped

FOR THE MARINADE
4 tbsp soy sauce
4 tbsp sweet chilli sauce
1 garlic clove, crushed
1 heaped tsp Chinese five spice powder
1 tsp light muscovado sugar
juice of 1 large lime

First make the marinade by placing all the ingredients in a bowl and mixing together well.

Using a meat mallet, rolling pin or the base of a saucepan, bash the steaks to make them a little thinner. Sit them in a large dish and spoon over 3 tablespoons of the marinade. Leave to marinate while you cook the noodles (see note).

Cook the noodles in boiling salted water according to the packet instructions, then drain and set aside.

Heat 2 tablespoons of the oil over a medium–high heat in a large non-stick frying pan. Season the marinated steaks with salt and pepper and fry for 1½–2 minutes on each side, then transfer to a warmed plate to rest.

Wipe the frying pan with a piece of kitchen paper, add the remaining oil and fry the red peppers and onion for 3–4 minutes over a high heat. Tip in the white parts of the Chinese leaves and fry for another minute. Add the remaining marinade and the drained noodles, toss until coated, then add the green parts of the Chinese leaves, some seasoning and half the coriander. Toss everything together to mix and heat through.

Divide the noodles between four plates. Very thinly slice the steaks and place on top of the noodles. Drizzle any resting steak juices on top and garnish with the remaining coriander to serve.

COOK'S NOTE
· Use your choice of steak; fillet would also be good but is more expensive than rump.
· If you have time, leave the beef to marinate for longer.

PREPARE AHEAD
Best made and served at once.

FREEZE
Not suitable for freezing.

Three Pestos

So versatile to use, pesto makes a wonderful, healthy full-bodied dip, sauce or spread. I've given you a choice of three.

SERVES 4 · PREP TIME: *10 minutes*

Classic Basil Pesto

50g (2oz) fresh basil, roughly chopped
1 garlic clove, sliced
50g (2oz) pine nuts, toasted (see note on page 29)
6 tbsp olive oil
50g (2oz) Parmesan or vegetarian hard cheese, grated

Coriander and Chilli Pesto

50g (2oz) fresh coriander, roughly chopped
½ fresh red chilli, deseeded and roughly chopped
50g (2oz) pine nuts, toasted (see note on page 29)
6 tbsp olive oil
juice of 1 small lime

Spinach and Walnut Pesto

50g (2oz) baby spinach, roughly torn
1 garlic clove, sliced
50g (2oz) walnut pieces, toasted (see note on page 29)
6 tbsp olive oil
juice of ½ lemon

Place all the ingredients in a small blender or mini food processor (see note) and season well with salt and pepper. Blend into a paste, scraping down the sides of the blender/ processor. Taste and adjust the seasoning if necessary.

COOK'S NOTE
It's quicker to use a small blender or mini food processor, but you can make these using a pestle and mortar, if you prefer – you just need strong arm muscles!

PREPARE AHEAD
Each pesto can be made ahead and kept in the fridge for up to 4 days in a sterilised jar (see page 282).

FREEZE
Pesto freezes well for up to a month.

Quick Pasta Sauces

Here are two delicious sauces that can be on the table in only 15 minutes.

SERVES 4 · PREP TIME: *5 minutes* · COOK TIME: *10 minutes*

Tomato and Basil Sauce

2 tbsp olive oil

1 large banana shallot, finely
    chopped

1 garlic clove, crushed

400g (14oz) passata

1 tbsp sun-dried tomato paste

2 tbsp chopped basil leaves

1 tsp caster sugar (or to taste)

Heat the oil in a small saucepan, then add the shallot and fry over a high heat for 2 minutes. Add the garlic and fry for 30 seconds, then add the passata and sun-dried tomato paste. Bring to the boil, reduce the heat and simmer for 5 minutes. Stir in the basil and season to taste with the sugar and some salt and pepper.

Creamy Bacon and Parmesan Sauce

1 tbsp olive oil

4 thick rashers of unsmoked
    back bacon, chopped

300ml (10fl oz) double cream

50g (2oz) Parmesan, finely
    grated

a squeeze of lemon juice

Heat the oil in a small frying pan. Add the bacon and fry over a high heat for 5 minutes until the fat has rendered and the bacon is lightly browned. Add the cream and bring to the boil, then reduce the heat and gently simmer for 1 minute. Remove from the heat and stir in the cheese to melt and a squeeze of lemon juice to cut through the richness. Season well with pepper, but be careful with the salt, as the bacon may already be quite salty.

COOK'S NOTE
Cook 350g (12oz) of dried pasta to serve with them.

PREPARE AHEAD
Both sauces may be made up to a day ahead.

FREEZE
Only the Tomato and Basil Sauce may be frozen.

Quick Veg

Cauliflower and Potato Cakes

Cauliflower is such a versatile vegetable. I love it pan-fried or roasted in the oven with other vegetables – recipes for both are included in my book *Classic*. This new recipe is for cauliflower cakes – so useful to make ahead or to keep in the freezer. They are perfect for lunch or to serve with roast beef.

MAKES 6 CAKES • PREP TIME: *15 minutes* • COOK TIME: *18–20 minutes*

350g (12oz) potatoes (such as Désirée, King Edward or Maris Piper), peeled and diced into 2cm (¾ in) cubes
a knob of butter
1 cauliflower (about 350g/12oz), broken into small florets
1 tbsp Dijon mustard
50g (2oz) mature Cheddar, grated
1 tbsp chopped parsley
50g (2oz) panko breadcrumbs (see note)
4 tbsp oil

Cook the potatoes in boiling salted water for 8–10 minutes or until tender, then drain and mash until smooth with the butter and some salt and pepper. Spoon into a bowl.

Meanwhile, cook the cauliflower in boiling salted water for 3–4 minutes or until tender, then drain and roughly chop into smaller pieces.

Tip the cauliflower into the bowl with the mashed potato and add the mustard, cheese, parsley and some seasoning. Shape into six cakes and coat in the breadcrumbs.

Heat the oil over a high heat and pan-fry the cakes in batches for 3–4 minutes on each side until they are piping hot and golden all over. Serve immediately.

COOK'S NOTE
Panko breadcrumbs are fine dried crumbs that give a very crispy coating. You can use fresh breadcrumbs instead, but you may need a few more.

PREPARE AHEAD
These can be prepared the day before (without the breadcrumbs) and kept in the fridge. Allow them to come up to room temperature before coating in the breadcrumbs and frying in batches.

FREEZE
The cauliflower cakes freeze well (without the breadcrumb coating).

Potato Cakes

Delicious and so versatile, these can be made from scratch or with leftover mashed potato. If you are using cold mash you may need to cook the potato cakes for a little longer to heat them through.

SERVES 4 · PREP TIME: *10 minutes* · COOK TIME: *20 minutes, plus cooling*

500g (1lb 2oz) potatoes (such as Désirée, King Edward or Maris Piper), peeled and chopped into 4cm (1½in) chunks
25g (1oz) butter
25g (1oz) panko breadcrumbs
2–3 tbsp olive oil

Cook the potatoes in a saucepan of boiling salted water for about 15 minutes or until tender. Drain, return to the pan to steam a little, then mash with the butter and season with salt and pepper. When cool enough to handle, shape into four even-sized balls, then flatten into cakes and coat in the breadcrumbs.

Heat a frying pan until hot, add the oil and fry over a high heat for about 2 minutes on each side, or until golden and piping hot.

Variations

Spring Onion Potato Cakes

Add six finely sliced spring onions and 2 teaspoons of grainy mustard to the seasoned mashed potato and beat well to mix in.

Leek and Potato Cakes

Rather than mixing the butter in with the mash, melt it in a small frying pan over a low heat, then fry one finely chopped medium leek for 3–4 minutes until soft but not browned. Mix in with the seasoned mashed potato, along with plenty of freshly ground black pepper.

Carrot and Ginger Potato Cakes

Peel and finely grate one medium carrot and a 2cm (¾in) knob of fresh root ginger and add to the seasoned mashed potato with 1 tablespoon of finely chopped coriander leaves. Beat well to combine.

Cheesy Potato Cakes

Finely grate 50g (2oz) of Parmesan and add to the seasoned mashed potato with 1 teaspoon of Dijon mustard, then beat well to combine.

PREPARE AHEAD

Can be made up to a day ahead. Shape the potato cakes and coat in the breadcrumbs, then keep covered in the fridge ready to cook when needed.

FREEZE

The potato cakes freeze well after coating and before frying. Wrap in greaseproof paper to keep them separate and to protect the breadcrumb coating. Put in a container, then defrost and fry when ready to eat.

Spiced Roasted Squash

So quick to make, this recipe uses spices that transform a simple side dish of squash into something rather special. Serve with a roast that you can cook alongside – or with a griddled steak or fish fillet.

SERVES 4 · PREP TIME: *10 minutes* · COOK TIME: *45 minutes*

1 large butternut squash, halved, deseeded and cubed (see note)
3 tbsp olive oil
1 tbsp ground cumin
1 tsp paprika
2 tbsp chopped fresh coriander

Preheat the oven to 200°c / 180°c Fan / Gas 6.

Place the squash in a roasting tin, drizzle over 2 tablespoons of the oil and season with salt and pepper. Sprinkle with half the cumin and roast in the oven for about 25 minutes until just tender.

Remove from the oven and sprinkle with the remaining cumin and the paprika, then return to the oven to roast for a further 20 minutes until tender and slightly browned at the edges.

Tip the roasted squash cubes into a serving dish. Drizzle with the remaining oil and scatter over the chopped coriander. Serve hot or cold.

COOK'S NOTE
You can save more time and buy pre-chopped squash, but it is more expensive.

PREPARE AHEAD
The squash can be roasted up to 4 hours ahead, then reheated in the oven to serve.

FREEZE
Not suitable for freezing.

French Buttered Potatoes

A tasty way to serve potatoes and very quick to cook – on the hob in just 20 minutes. Use vegetable stock for a vegetarian option.

SERVES 4 · PREP TIME: *10 minutes* · COOK TIME: *20 minutes*

2 tbsp sunflower oil
25g (1oz) butter
1 onion, finely sliced
500g (1lb 2oz) baby new
  potatoes (unpeeled –
  see note), thinly sliced
  (no more than
  1cm / ½in thick)
200ml (7fl oz) vegetable or
  chicken stock
1 tbsp fresh lemon juice
2 tbsp chopped parsley

Heat the oil in a large frying pan over a high heat and add the butter. When foaming, add the onion and potatoes and gently stir over the heat until coated. Cover with a lid and cook over a medium heat for about 10 minutes.

Pour in the stock, cover again with the lid and cook for another 10 minutes, or until the potatoes are tender when tested with the point of a knife.

Remove the lid and increase the heat to drive off some of the liquid and finish cooking. Season with salt and pepper and add the lemon juice and parsley. Toss carefully and serve in a warmed serving dish.

COOK'S NOTE
Keep the skin on the baby new potatoes – it is so thin and easy to eat and makes the preparation far quicker. It also helps the potato slices to keep their shape during cooking.

PREPARE AHEAD
Can be made up to 3 hours ahead and reheated in the pan or in a hot oven to serve.

FREEZE
Not suitable for freezing.

Double Potato and Squash Roasties

Roasties are such a favourite; chopping up the vegetables doesn't take long and the smaller pieces cook in less time. This dish would work well with parsnips too.

SERVES 4 · PREP TIME: *10 minutes* · COOK TIME: *25 minutes*

3 tbsp sunflower oil

250g (9oz) sweet potatoes, peeled and diced into 1.5cm (⅝in) cubes

250g (9oz) baby new potatoes (unpeeled), diced into 1.5cm (⅝in) cubes

350g (9oz) butternut squash, peeled, deseeded and diced into 1.5cm (⅝in) cubes

1 tbsp chopped thyme leaves

1 tbsp chopped rosemary leaves

Preheat the oven to 200°c / 180°c Fan / Gas 6.

Measure the oil into a large, shallow roasting tin and place in the oven for 5 minutes to get hot.

When the oil in the roasting tin is hot, carefully add the vegetables to the tin, spreading them out in a single layer (see note). Season with salt and pepper and turn to coat well in the hot oil. Roast in the oven for about 20 minutes, then turn the veg and shake the tin to spread out the pieces again in an even layer.

Sprinkle over the herbs and return to the oven for another 5 minutes until crisp and golden.

Serve hot with any roast you wish.

COOK'S NOTE

For ease and speed, put all the uncooked diced vegetables in a large bowl, season with salt and pepper and mix well before tipping into the tin and spreading in a single layer so that they roast evenly.

PREPARE AHEAD

Can be prepared up to 6 hours ahead and roasted to serve.

FREEZE

Not suitable for freezing.

Garlic Creamed Spinach

Sometimes forgotten as a side dish, spinach is so quick to cook and, with a little cream, it's extra-special too.

SERVES 3–4 · PREP TIME: *2 minutes* · COOK TIME: *5 minutes*

1 tbsp olive oil

2 garlic cloves, crushed

250g (9oz) baby spinach
   (see note)

2–3 tbsp double cream
   (to taste)

¼ tsp freshly grated nutmeg

Heat the oil over a high heat in a large frying pan. Add the garlic and fry for 30 seconds, then add the spinach and toss for 2 minutes until the leaves have just wilted (see note). Add the cream and nutmeg and stir until heated through. Season well with salt and pepper and spoon into a heated dish to serve.

COOK'S NOTES
- Baby spinach is more tender than more mature spinach so cooks quicker. Plus, it does not have the tough woody stems that need removing, reducing the prep time.
- If the mountain of raw spinach in the pan is a bit tricky to stir at first, use two wooden spoons to toss it. It will get easier to stir as the leaves start to wilt down.

PREPARE AHEAD
Best made and served immediately.

FREEZE
Not suitable for freezing

Spinach, Cabbage and Mushroom Stir-Fry

Fresh and flavoursome, this is wonderful on its own or as a side dish with meat or fish. It is also perfect for vegetarians – the mushrooms make it very substantial and are a great substitute for meat.

SERVES 4–6 · PREP TIME: *10 minutes* · **COOK TIME:** *10 minutes*

2 tbsp olive oil

a knob of butter

1 onion, thinly sliced

250g (9oz) chestnut mushrooms, thickly sliced

200g (7oz) oyster mushrooms, cut in half lengthways

1 garlic clove, crushed

½ Hispi cabbage, core removed and leaves shredded (see note)

150g (5oz) baby spinach

Heat the oil and butter in a large frying pan or wok. Add the onion and fry over a high heat for a few minutes. Stir in the mushrooms, then cover with a lid, reduce the heat and cook for 2 minutes. Remove the lid and brown over a high heat for a minute or so until golden. Add the garlic and fry for 30 seconds, then add the cabbage and stir-fry for 2–3 minutes, tossing over the heat. Tip in the spinach and toss in the pan until wilted.

Season well with salt and pepper and serve at once in a large bowl.

COOK'S NOTE
Hispi cabbage, also known as pointed cabbage or pointed spring cabbage, is a favourite of mine. With firm leaves that hold their shape in the pan, it stir-fries really well. It also keeps well in the fridge for up to a week – just remove any outer leaves that become a little tired.

PREPARE AHEAD
Prepare the vegetables up to 2 hours in advance. Keep the cabbage fresh in a bag until ready to fry and just tip it straight into the pan.

FREEZE
Not suitable for freezing.

Stir-Fried Pak Choi with Soy and Sugar Snap Peas

A quick, healthy stir-fry – fresh, with a slight saltiness from the soy. This is lovely served as an accompaniment to salmon.

SERVES 4 • PREP TIME: *5 minutes* • COOK TIME: *3–4 minutes*

1 tbsp sunflower oil

225g (8oz) pak choi, root trimmed and sliced into quarters through the root

200g (7oz) sugar snap peas, string removed if necessary and halved lengthways (see note)

1 tbsp soy sauce

Place the oil in a large frying pan over a high heat. Add the vegetables and stir-fry for 3–4 minutes until the leaves wilt and the sugar snaps and pak choi stems soften.

Take off the heat and add the soy (it will sizzle and spit in the hot pan), then grind over some black pepper and serve immediately.

COOK'S NOTE
Cutting the sugar snaps in half lengthways means they cook more quickly and they also show the lovely peas inside.

PREPARE AHEAD
Make and serve immediately.

FREEZE
Not suitable for freezing.

Vegetable Kebabs

Cut the vegetables into pieces roughly the same size so they cook at the same rate. Shop-bought pesto is a great store-cupboard standby, but fresh pesto is tastier. Try using a teaspoon of one of the Three Pestos on page 190. These kebabs would be great cooked on the barbecue too. Serve as a side with meat or with the Cabbage and Fennel Slaw on page 74.

SERVES 6 *as a side* · **PREP TIME:** *20 minutes* · **COOK TIME:** *12 minutes*

12 small chestnut mushrooms
½ small cauliflower, broken into small florets
1 small red pepper, deseeded and sliced into squares
4 mini courgettes, cut into slices about 1.5cm (⅝in) thick (see note)
2 tbsp olive oil
½ garlic clove, crushed
1 tsp pesto (see recipe introduction)
1 tsp runny honey

Preheat the oven to 220°C/200°C Fan/Gas 7 and line a baking sheet with baking paper. Leave six wooden skewers to soak in cold water for 10 minutes.

Thread the mushrooms and cauliflower on to the skewers with alternating pieces of red pepper and courgette (see note), then place on the prepared baking sheet.

Mix the oil, garlic, pesto and honey together in a small bowl. Season with salt and pepper and brush the assembled skewers with the mixture.

Cook in the oven for about 12 minutes or until the vegetables are cooked, lightly golden and slightly charred at the edges.

COOK'S NOTES
· If mini courgettes are not available, cut a larger courgette into quarters lengthways and then into 1–2cm (½–¾ in) chunks.
· Leave a little space between each piece of vegetable so that it cooks more quickly. Thread the cauliflower florets through the head and stalk, so that they don't fall off.

PREPARE AHEAD
The kebabs can be assembled up to 6 hours ahead.

FREEZE
Not suitable for freezing.

Pan-Fried Little Gem Lettuce

Pan-frying lettuce is an old-fashioned technique, but it tastes really delicious. These Little Gems could even be cooked on a barbecue – just brush with oil and cook until golden and charred. Perfect with fish, such as the Sea Bass en Papillote with Courgette Ribbons on page 108.

SERVES 2–4 · PREP TIME: *5 minutes* · COOK TIME: *3–5 minutes*

2 large Little Gem lettuces
  (see note)
1 tbsp sunflower oil
a large knob of butter

Trim the base of the lettuces and remove any loose outer leaves. Slice into quarters lengthways through the stem so that the leaves hold together.

Place a large frying pan over a medium–high heat. Add the oil and butter and, when the butter is foaming, add the lettuce wedges. Fry for 3–5 minutes, turning occasionally, until a nutty brown colour all over. You want them to be well coloured but still holding their shape and keeping some crunch.

Season with salt and pepper and serve hot.

COOK'S NOTE
Little Gems are the ideal lettuce for this dish as they hold their shape when heated.

PREPARE AHEAD
Make and serve immediately.

FREEZE
Not suitable for freezing.

Chargrilled Aubergines

Aubergines are one of my favourite vegetables. This recipe is very simple and goes perfectly with the Spiced Lentils with Pickled Ginger on page 85.

perfectly with the Spiced Lentils with Pickled Ginger on page 85.

SERVES 4–6 · PREP TIME: *10 minutes* **· COOK TIME:** *4–6 minutes per batch*

2 small aubergines, cut into slices 1cm (½in) thick (see note)
4 tbsp olive oil
2 tbsp balsamic vinegar
1 tbsp chopped marjoram

Put the sliced aubergines in a bowl, add the olive oil and toss together until all the slices are well coated. Season with salt and pepper.

Heat a griddle pan until very hot (see note). Add the slices in a single layer and chargrill over a high heat for 2–3 minutes on each side until just soft and with dark griddle marks. You will need to do this in batches.

Arrange the slices on a platter, pour over the balsamic vinegar and scatter with the marjoram to serve.

COOK'S NOTES
· If only larger, older aubergines are available, you may need to 'degorge' them first: sprinkle the aubergine slices with salt and leave them for 30 minutes to draw out the bitter juices, then rinse off the salt before cooking the slices.
· The pan needs to be very hot to drive off any juices and ensure that the aubergine slices stay dry and don't become soggy. If you don't have a griddle pan, use a heavy-based frying pan instead.

PREPARE AHEAD
Can be made up to 4 hours ahead and reheated to serve. The aubergines are also good served cold.

FREEZE
Not suitable for freezing.

Cauliflower, Aubergine and Lemon Grass Thai Curry

Perfect for non-meat eaters, this is full of vegetables and has a creamy, aromatic flavour. Thai curry is traditionally much thinner than the Indian variety, so don't expect this to be thick.

SERVES 4 · PREP TIME: *10 minutes* · COOK TIME: *15–20 minutes*

2 tbsp sunflower oil
2 banana shallots, sliced
½ fresh red chilli, deseeded and sliced
2 garlic cloves, crushed
2cm (¾in) knob of fresh root ginger, peeled and grated (see note on page 114)
1 tsp curry powder
1 sweet potato, peeled and cut into 2cm (¾in) pieces
2 × 400ml tins of full-fat coconut milk
2 lemon grass stalks, bashed
1 small cauliflower, broken into tiny florets (see note)
1 aubergine, chopped into 2cm (¾in) dice
2 tsp fish sauce
1 tbsp sweet chilli sauce
juice of ½ lemon
1 bunch of coriander, chopped

Heat the oil in a wide-based frying pan over a high heat. Tip in the shallots, chilli, garlic and ginger and fry for 2 minutes. Add the curry powder and sweet potato and stir everything until well combined. Add the coconut milk and the lemon grass stalks and stir to mix well. Bring to the boil, then cover with a lid, reduce the heat and simmer for 5 minutes.

Add the cauliflower and aubergine and continue to simmer for another 5–10 minutes until all the vegetables are soft.

Remove the lemon grass and discard. Stir in the fish sauce, sweet chilli sauce, lemon juice and half the coriander. Season to taste with salt and pepper and serve with steamed rice and the remaining coriander scattered over.

COOK'S NOTE
Keep all the cauliflower florets the same size so they cook at the same rate.

PREPARE AHEAD
Can be made up to 6 hours ahead and gently reheated.

FREEZE
Not suitable for freezing.

Puddings

Gooseberry and Elderflower Fool

A fool is an old-fashioned dessert but it always goes down well. So easy to make and perfect for using up home-grown produce. The fruit purée is usually mixed with just cream, but I like the addition of yoghurt as it makes it slightly less rich.

SERVES 6–8 · PREP TIME: *15 minutes* · COOK TIME: *5 minutes, plus chilling*

500g (1lb 2oz) gooseberries
100g (4oz) caster sugar
3–4 tbsp elderflower cordial (to taste)
300ml (10fl oz) double cream
100g (4oz) thick Greek-style natural yoghurt or crème fraîche
mint leaves, to decorate (optional)

You will need 6–8 glasses or ceramic pots/ramekins.

Measure the gooseberries, sugar and elderflower cordial into a medium saucepan and mix well. Place over a high heat and cook for about 5 minutes, stirring until the sugar has dissolved and the fruit is soft. Blitz with a hand blender and then push the purée through a sieve to remove the skins, tops and tails. Set aside to cool.

Reserve 6–8 teaspoons of the cooled gooseberry purée to decorate.

Whisk the cream to soft peaks and fold in the yoghurt or crème fraîche. Carefully stir in the cooled purée until well combined, then divide the fool between your chosen containers (see note). Leave in the fridge for a minimum of 2 hours to set.

Spoon 1 teaspoon of the reserved gooseberry purée on top of each of the fools and decorate with mint leaves, if using, to serve.

COOK'S NOTE
For quick and easy portioning, decant the fool into a jug and pour into the glasses or pots/ramekins. Take care to wipe the sides of the containers to remove any spillages before the dessert thickens.

PREPARE AHEAD
Can be made up to a day ahead and stored in the fridge; bring up to room temperature to serve.

FREEZE
Not suitable for freezing.

Oven-Baked Peaches
with Marsala and Almonds

Quick and delicious, this would suit any occasion – a family meal or a dinner party. The sweet peach juices mingle with the Marsala, while the almonds and amaretti biscuits add crunch and flavour. This recipe would also work well with apricots, plums or nectarines.

SERVES 6 · PREP TIME: *10 minutes* · COOK TIME: *20 minutes*

6 ripe but firm peaches,
   halved (see note)
6 tbsp Marsala (see note)
50g (2oz) amaretti biscuits
3 tbsp demerara sugar
25g (1oz) butter, plus extra
   for greasing
25g (1oz) flaked almonds

Preheat the oven to 200°C/180°C Fan/Gas 6 and grease a shallow ovenproof dish.

Arrange the peach halves, cut side up, in the prepared dish and spoon over 4 tablespoons of the Marsala. Place the amaretti in a freezer bag and use a rolling pin to crush into fine crumbs.

Measure the sugar and butter into a small bowl and add the crushed biscuits, then rub together using your fingertips into a crumble-like mixture. Spread the mixture over the peaches, making sure each peach half is covered with the topping, and sprinkle with the flaked almonds.

Bake for about 15 minutes, then remove from the oven and spoon over the remaining 2 tablespoons of Marsala. Return to the oven to cook for another 5 minutes or until soft and golden. Serve warm with cream.

COOK'S NOTES
- Choose peaches that are just under-ripe, not too soft, so that they keep their shape when cooked. The quickest way to prepare the peaches is to cut around each peach to the stone and twist both halves to separate them. Use a small sharp knife to carefully cut around the stone if it doesn't come out immediately.
- If you haven't any Marsala, use brandy instead. The almond flavour of amaretto would also go well with this dish.

PREPARE AHEAD
The peaches can be marinated in the Marsala an hour or so in advance. Make the topping ahead but sprinkle over just before cooking so that it keeps its crunch.

FREEZE
Not suitable for freezing.

Upside-Down Rhubarb Pudding with Caramel Sauce

Hearty and warming, upside-down pudding is so simple to prepare, especially as the sponge uses an all-in-one method. You must use young, pink rhubarb at the start of the season as the older, green variety would be too tart. Forced rhubarb from Yorkshire is available in the early part of the year – January to March.

SERVES 6–8 · PREP TIME: *20 minutes* · COOK TIME: *50–60 minutes, plus cooling*

700g (1lb 9oz) pink rhubarb, sliced into 2cm (¾in) pieces (see recipe introduction)

FOR THE CARAMEL SAUCE
175g (6oz) caster sugar
100g (4oz) butter, diced
4 tbsp double cream

FOR THE SPONGE
2 large eggs
100g (4oz) self-raising flour
100g (4oz) butter, softened
100g (4oz) caster sugar
1 tsp vanilla extract

You will need a 23cm (9in) round, deep cake tin with a fixed base. Preheat the oven to 180°c/160°c Fan/Gas 4.

First make the caramel sauce. Put the sugar into a saucepan with 4 tablespoons of water and stir over a low heat until dissolved. When the mixture is completely clear, increase the heat and boil for 5–10 minutes without stirring, until caramel coloured. Remove from the heat and add the butter, stirring until you have a thick caramel. Add the cream and stir until the sauce is the consistency of thick syrup. Take care as it will splutter and bubble.

Allow the bubbling to subside, then pour the caramel into the base of the tin. Arrange some of the rhubarb in a neat layer on top, then scatter over the rest. Set aside to cool.

Meanwhile, measure all the sponge ingredients into a large bowl. Beat with an electric hand whisk until light and fluffy. Spoon on top of the rhubarb and spread out to the edges to cover the fruit. Bake for about 45–50 minutes, until well risen and coming away from the sides of the tin.

Leave for about 5–10 minutes to settle and to allow the tin to become cool enough to handle before inverting on to a pudding plate that's large enough to hold any extra toffee sauce. Serve warm with cream or crème fraîche.

COOK'S NOTE
Make this with other fruits in season, such as apricots or plums, stoned and halved and placed cut side down in the caramel so that they appear cut side up when the cake is turned out.

PREPARE AHEAD
Can be made up to 4 hours ahead and kept, covered, in the fridge, ready to bake.

FREEZE
The cooked pudding freezes well.

Glazed Pineapple with Rum and Lime

Such a speedy, healthy pudding – perfect for camping or indeed any al fresco meal!
Serve with Rum and Raisin Ice Cream (see page 234) for an extra treat.

SERVES 4 · PREP TIME: *15 minutes* · COOK TIME: *2 minutes*

1 medium-sized ripe pineapple
3 tbsp light muscovado sugar
3 tbsp rum
juice of ½ lime

Remove the base and top of the pineapple with a sharp knife and slice off the skin. Cut the pineapple lengthways into eight wedges, then remove and discard the core.

Heat a large griddle pan until very hot (see note).

Mix the sugar and rum together in a small bowl. Brush the rum glaze all over the pineapple wedges, then place in the pan and chargrill for 1 minute on each side or until golden and with griddle marks on the fruit.

Squeeze over the lime juice and any extra rum syrup to serve.

COOK'S NOTE
Make sure the pan is very hot – you just want to glaze the pineapple, not cook it, as it should still be firm when you eat it. Use a heavy-based frying pan if you don't have a griddle pan.

PREPARE AHEAD
Best made and served immediately.

FREEZE
Not suitable for freezing.

Passion Fruit and Orange Cheesecake

Quick, light and simple – with no gelatine! Use oat biscuits as a variation if you like a textured cheesecake base.

SERVES 6–8 · PREP TIME: *15 minutes, plus chilling* · COOK TIME: *2 minutes*

FOR THE BASE
150g (5oz) digestive biscuits
75g (3oz) butter, plus extra
  for greasing

FOR THE TOPPING
4 passion fruit, halved
250g (9oz) full-fat mascarpone
  cheese (see note)
½ × 325g jar of good-quality
  orange curd
zest of 1 orange: ½ finely
  grated and ½ sliced into
  very thin strips
200ml (7fl oz) pouring double
  cream, lightly whipped

You will need a 20cm (8in) round, spring-form cake tin. Grease the tin and line the base with a disc of baking paper.

First make the cheesecake base. Place the biscuits on a board and use a rolling pin to crush into fine crumbs. Melt the butter in a wide-based pan over a medium heat. Remove from the heat, add the crushed biscuits and stir until well mixed. Press into the base of the tin (not up the sides).

Place the flesh of two of the passion fruit in a sieve set over a bowl and use a wooden spoon to push the pulp through the sieve so that the juice collects in the bowl. Discard the seeds left in the sieve. Add the mascarpone, orange curd and grated orange zest to the juice in the bowl and mix together using an electric hand whisk until well combined. Fold in the whipped cream.

Spoon the mixture into the tin on top of the biscuit base and level the top. Chill in the fridge for a minimum of 4 hours, or preferably overnight, to firm up.

Decorate the top of the cheesecake with the seeds and pulp of the remaining two passion fruit and with the thin strips of orange zest. Carefully release from the tin and place on a cake stand or plate to serve.

COOK'S NOTE
Full-fat mascarpone helps the cheesecake set; the low-fat version would be too soft.

PREPARE AHEAD
The cheesecake itself can be made and chilled up to a day ahead without the decoration. Decorate up to 2 hours before serving.

FREEZE
Not suitable for freezing.

Rum and Raisin Ice Cream

Sweet, naughty and delicious, this has a gorgeously smooth and silky texture. With no churning required, it is so straightforward to make too. Condensed milk is the magic ingredient here – the thick, rich combination of sugar and milk helps to prevent any ice crystals from forming and makes the ice cream easy to scoop straight from the freezer. Soaking the raisins overnight is worth doing as this plumps them up so they are juicy. Without soaking, they would be hard to eat.

MAKES 1 LITRE · PREP TIME: *15 minutes, plus soaking* · **FREEZE TIME:** *12 hours or overnight*

150g (5oz) raisins
50ml (2fl oz) dark rum
300ml (10fl oz) pouring double cream
1 × 397g tin of full-fat condensed milk

You will need a 1-litre (1¾-pint) freezer-proof container or eight ramekins (see note).

Place the raisins in a saucepan. Add the rum and gently heat it until just boiling. Spoon into a bowl, then cover and leave to soak overnight until all the raisins are plump and the rum has been absorbed (see recipe introduction).

Pour the cream into a large bowl and whisk into soft peaks using an electric hand whisk. Carefully fold in the condensed milk, then the raisins and any excess rum and mix well.

Spoon into the freezer-proof container or ramekins and freeze for a minimum of 12 hours or overnight.

Serve scoops of ice cream with fresh fruit like the Glazed Pineapple with Rum and Lime (see page 231).

COOK'S NOTE
Spooned into ramekins, the ice cream will freeze more quickly – in just a few hours. Don't overfill them as the mixture will expand as it freezes – ramekins with a capacity of 150ml (5fl oz) would be ideal.

PREPARE AHEAD
Make the ice cream at least 12 hours ahead.

FREEZE
Freezes for up to 2 months.

Blackberry and Custard Money Bags

These filo parcels look a bit like old-fashioned money bags, or the bag
Dick Whittington carried on the end of his stick – hence the name.

MAKES 6 · PREP TIME: *20 minutes* **· COOK TIME:** *15 minutes*

250g (9oz) full-fat mascarpone
    cheese
50g (2oz) caster sugar
1 tsp vanilla extract
1 × 270g packet of filo pastry
    (see note)
50g (2oz) butter, melted, plus
    extra for greasing
6 tbsp ground almonds
    (see note)
300g (11oz) fresh blackberries,
    hulled
icing sugar, for dusting

Preheat the oven to 200°C/180°C Fan/Gas 6, then lightly grease
a baking sheet or line with baking paper.

To make a quick custard-style sauce, measure the mascarpone
into a bowl, add the sugar and vanilla extract and mix together
until well combined and the sugar no longer feels grainy.

Lay the pastry sheets on a work surface. Cut into 12 squares each
measuring about 20 × 20cm (8 × 8in), then set aside, covered with
a clean, damp tea towel, to prevent the pastry from drying out.

Take one square of pastry and brush with melted butter. Put
1 tablespoon of the ground almonds in the middle then place
one-sixth of the blackberries on top. Spoon one-sixth of the
mascarpone custard on top of the berries. Fold one side of the
pastry over the filling, then fold the opposite side over the top.
Fold one open end underneath and then tuck the other end
underneath as well. Repeat with five of the remaining squares
of pastry and the remaining fillings.

Once you have made all six parcels, take another square of
pastry and wrap it around one of the parcels to form a money
bag, making sure the custard is at the top. Scrunch the edges of
the filo together at the top to make the 'bag' and repeat with the
remaining five parcels. Place them carefully on the prepared
baking sheet, leaving plenty of space around each one, and brush
with melted butter. Cook for about 15 minutes or until the pastry
is golden and crisp.

Dust with icing sugar and serve with a little cream.

COOK'S NOTES

- Different makes of filo pastry come in different sizes, so you may find you have some pastry left over. It freezes well, however.
- The almonds in each parcel soak up any excess liquid; if you have a nut allergy, use the same quantity of breadcrumbs instead.

PREPARE AHEAD

Can be assembled up to 6 hours ahead and baked to serve.

FREEZE

Not suitable for freezing.

Pear, Ginger and Almond Brioche Tart

Many moons ago I created a brioche tart with apricots. It is a recipe many people still say is one of their favourites, so I have made a new version using pears and almonds. Take time to arrange the pears beautifully on the top of the brioche. It helps to make the tart look really stunning – guaranteed to impress!

SERVES 6–8 · PREP TIME: *10–15 minutes* · COOK TIME: *30–35 minutes, plus resting*

butter, softened, for greasing

½ brioche loaf

1 egg, beaten

250g (9oz) full-fat mascarpone cheese

2 tbsp caster sugar

1 tsp vanilla extract

4 stem ginger pieces, finely chopped

2 × 400g tins of pears, drained, dried and thinly sliced (see note)

3 tbsp ginger syrup (from the stem ginger jar)

25g (1oz) flaked almonds

You will need a 28cm (11in) round shallow dish. Preheat the oven to 200°C/180°C Fan/Gas 6 and grease the base and sides of the dish.

Cut the brioche into slices 1cm (½in) thick and arrange in the base of the prepared dish, placing the slices close together and cutting them, if necessary, to fit the base.

Mix the egg and mascarpone together in a bowl with the sugar and vanilla extract. Fold in the ginger pieces and then spoon into the dish to cover the brioche in an even layer. Arrange the pear slices over the top in a spiral pattern. Brush the pears with the ginger syrup and then sprinkle with the flaked almonds.

Bake in the oven for 30–35 minutes until lightly golden on top and underneath. Remove from the oven and leave to sit for 10 minutes before serving warm with cream or crème fraîche.

COOK'S NOTE

If fresh pears are in season, peel and thinly slice your favourite variety. If using tinned pears, lay the drained fruit on a plate lined with kitchen paper to soak up any excess liquid.

PREPARE AHEAD

The tart can be assembled up to 4 hours ahead and baked to serve.

FREEZE

Not suitable for freezing.

Limoncello Trifle

Such a speedy dessert, this is a new favourite! Serve the trifle in a shallow, wide-based dish so that the layers are even, and every spoonful has a mixture of all the flavours. Use a glass dish, if you can, so everyone can see the layers.

SERVES 6 · PREP TIME: *15 minutes, plus chilling*

300g (11oz) fresh raspberries
6 trifle sponges (see note)
4 tbsp lemon curd
10 tbsp limoncello
250g (9oz) full-fat mascarpone cheese
1 × 300ml tub of fresh vanilla custard or home-made custard (see page 251)
finely grated zest of ½ large lemon

You will need a 1.4-litre (2½-pint) trifle dish (preferably glass, see recipe introduction). Arrange the raspberries in the base of the dish.

Slice the sponges in half horizontally, spread one half generously with lemon curd and then sandwich the halves back together. Cut each sandwich in half lengthways to give two fingers. Arrange the sandwiches around the edge and in the centre of the dish, covering the raspberries, with their cut sides facing outwards, so you can see them through the glass.

Drizzle over the limoncello, soaking the sponges well.

Measure the mascarpone into a large bowl. Mix gently using an electric hand whisk until softened, then carefully add the custard, a little at a time, until it is fully incorporated and the mixture is smooth. Pour the custard over the sponges and level the top. Sprinkle over the lemon zest.

Chill until needed and remove from the fridge 10 minutes before serving to bring back up to room temperature.

COOK'S NOTE
Trifle sponges are softer than sponge fingers, which makes them quicker and easier to spread with the lemon curd and then sandwich back together.

PREPARE AHEAD
Can be made up to 8 hours ahead and kept chilled in the fridge.

FREEZE
Not suitable for freezing.

Indulgent Chocolate Surprise

This is a chocolate sponge with a surprise chocolate sauce. Don't be alarmed by the amount of water used in the recipe. The rich sauce will magically appear bubbling under the baked surface of the sponge once it is cooked.

SERVES 6 · PREP TIME: *10 minutes* · COOK TIME: *25 minutes*

FOR THE SPONGE
60g (2oz) caster sugar
60g (2oz) semolina
30g (1oz) cocoa powder, sifted
1 tsp baking powder
30g (1oz) butter, melted, plus
    extra for greasing
2 eggs
icing sugar, for dusting

FOR THE SAUCE
100g (4oz) light muscovado
    sugar
2 tbsp cocoa powder, sifted
300ml (10fl oz) boiling water

You will need a wide-based, deep ovenproof dish about 1.2 litres (2 pints) in capacity. Preheat the oven to 180°c/160°c Fan/Gas 6 and grease the dish well.

To make the sponge, measure the caster sugar and semolina into a bowl with the cocoa powder and baking powder. Mix the melted butter and eggs in a jug and beat with a fork until blended. Pour this mixture into the bowl with the dry ingredients (see note) and whisk carefully with an electric hand whisk on a low setting until combined and smooth, taking care not to overbeat the mixture. Spoon into the prepared dish and level the surface.

Measure all the ingredients for the sauce into a bowl and mix until smooth. Pour over the sponge mixture. Bake in the oven for about 25 minutes or until well risen on top and the sauce is bubbling underneath.

Dust with icing sugar and serve with cream.

COOK'S NOTE
It is important to keep the dry and wet ingredients separate until mixing.

PREPARE AHEAD
Assemble the uncooked sponge in the dish up to 4 hours ahead. Pour over the sauce just before baking.

FREEZE
Not suitable for freezing.

Chocolate Cappuccino Tart

An indulgent, rich chocolate tart – quick to make and even quicker to devour! Like
a cup of cappuccino, it has a creamy topping and scattering of chocolate shavings.

SERVES 8–10 · PREP TIME: *15 minutes, plus chilling* **· COOK TIME:** *5 minutes*

FOR THE BASE
50g (2oz) dark chocolate,
  broken into pieces
75g (3oz) butter
15 digestive biscuits, finely
  crushed

FOR THE FILLING
350g (12oz) dark chocolate,
  broken into pieces
100g (4oz) butter
1 heaped tsp instant coffee
  granules dissolved in 1 tsp
  boiling water
250ml (9fl oz) double cream
200g (7oz) full-fat crème
  fraîche (see note)

TO DECORATE
150ml (5fl oz) double cream,
  lightly whipped
chocolate shavings or coarsely
  grated chocolate

You will need a 23cm (9in) round, loose-bottomed, fluted tart tin
with deep sides and a piping bag with a plain nozzle (optional).

To make the base, melt the chocolate and butter in a wide-based
pan over a medium heat (see note). Remove the pan from the heat,
add the crushed biscuits and stir to combine. Press into the base
of the tart tin and chill in the fridge while you make the filling.

To make the filling, place the chocolate and butter in a large
heatproof bowl and add the coffee and double cream. Set the
bowl over a pan of just simmering water and heat until runny,
stirring gently until smooth. Remove from the heat and allow
to cool down a little, then mix in the crème fraîche by hand.
Carefully pour the mixture into the tin on top of the biscuit base
and chill for a minimum of 2 hours, or ideally overnight, until set.

Remove the tart from the tin and place it on a cake stand or plate.
Serve straight from the fridge.

To decorate, spoon the whipped cream into a piping bag (if using)
and pipe or dollop five large blobs of the cream into the middle
of the tart. Sprinkle over the chocolate shavings or grated
chocolate and serve in thin slices.

COOK'S NOTES
· You'll need full-fat crème fraîche for this recipe
  to help the filling set.
· Be sure not to overheat the chocolate and butter
  mixture – heat it until it is just warm enough
  to melt.

PREPARE AHEAD
Can be made up to a day ahead and kept in the
fridge. Decorate 2 hours before serving.

FREEZE
Not suitable for freezing.

Piccoli Tiramisù

A classic Italian dessert, this is still a favourite of mine. I've made individual puddings here (*piccolo* means 'small' in Italian), as they set more quickly, but you could make this in a large 1.2-litre (2-pint) dish, if you prefer.

SERVES 4–6 · PREP TIME: *20 minutes, plus chilling*

250g (9oz) full-fat mascarpone cheese
300ml (10fl oz) double cream
2 tsp vanilla extract
4 tbsp icing sugar, sifted
125ml (4fl oz) strong coffee, cooled
6 tbsp brandy
12 sponge fingers (see note)
50g (2oz) dark chocolate, coarsely grated

You will need 4–6 small tumblers.

Measure the mascarpone and about 50ml (2fl oz) of the cream into a large bowl, whisking until smooth. Slowly add the remaining cream and whisk again into soft peaks, being careful not to over-mix or it will be too thick. Fold in the vanilla extract and icing sugar.

Meanwhile, in a separate bowl, combine the coffee and brandy.

Break six of the sponge fingers in half and dip into the coffee and brandy mixture (see note). Arrange the soaked sponge fingers in the base of the tumblers. Spoon half of the cream mixture on top and half of the grated chocolate.

Break the remaining sponge fingers and soak in the coffee and brandy. Place on the cream layer, then spoon the remaining cream mixture on top, levelling neatly.

Chill for a few hours, if possible, then sprinkle with the remaining chocolate before serving at room temperature.

COOK'S NOTES
· If you can't find sponge fingers, use trifle sponges or slices of sponge cake instead, though they are less robust once dipped, so take care when assembling.
· Give the sponge fingers a really good dunking in the coffee and brandy. There's plenty to go around and, ideally, you want them to absorb all the flavour and add moisture to the dish.

PREPARE AHEAD
Make up to 8 hours ahead and store in the fridge.

FREEZE
Not suitable for freezing.

Quick Sauces for Puddings

Adding a homemade sauce to a bowl of ice cream makes even the simplest of puddings a real treat. I love the Raspberry Coulis poured over mango sorbet.

Chocolate Fudge Sauce

SERVES 4–6 • PREP TIME: *5 minutes* • COOK TIME: *5 minutes*

100g (4oz) butter, cubed
200g (7oz) light muscovado sugar
125ml (4fl oz) double cream
100g (4oz) dark chocolate, broken into pieces

Place the butter, sugar and cream in a saucepan over a low heat and stir until the butter has melted and the mixture is smooth, then increase the heat and boil for 1–2 minutes, stirring constantly. Remove from the heat, add the chocolate and stir until it has melted and the sauce is smooth and shiny (see note). Serve warm.

White Chocolate Sauce

SERVES 4–6 • PREP TIME: *5 minutes* • COOK TIME: *5 minutes, plus cooling*

150g (5oz) good-quality white chocolate (ideally Belgian or Swiss), broken into pieces
300ml (10fl oz) double cream

Place the chocolate and cream in a bowl set over a pan of just simmering water and gently melt until runny and warm, taking care not to overheat the chocolate. Remove from the heat and leave to cool and thicken a little. Serve warm.

Toffee Sauce

SERVES 4–6 • PREP TIME: *5 minutes* • COOK TIME: *5 minutes*

300ml (10fl oz) double cream
75g (3oz) butter, cubed
100g (4oz) light muscovado sugar

Measure all the ingredients into a medium saucepan and place over a medium heat. Stir until the butter has melted and the sugar has dissolved, then boil for 3–5 minutes until thickened (see note). Serve warm as a toffee sauce or cooled as a fudgy spread.

Raspberry Coulis

SERVES 4–6 · PREP TIME: *5 minutes*

600g (1lb 5oz) fresh or frozen
    (and defrosted) raspberries
    (see freeze note)
75g (3oz) icing sugar

Measure the ingredients into a food processor and whizz until smooth. Pour into a large-holed sieve or strainer set over a bowl and strain out the pips.

Fresh Vanilla Custard

SERVES 4–6 · PREP TIME: *5 minutes* · COOK TIME: *5–8 minutes*

2 large eggs
1 large egg yolk
2 heaped tsp cornflour
25g (1oz) caster sugar
3 tsp vanilla extract
500ml (18fl oz) full-fat milk

Break the whole eggs into a large heatproof mixing bowl, add the egg yolk, cornflour, sugar and vanilla and whisk by hand until combined.

Pour the milk into a pan and place over a gentle heat until hand hot. Slowly pour the hot milk over the egg mixture, whisking continuously until combined.

Pour back into the pan and return to a gentle heat (see note). Stir continuously with a wooden spatula until just thickened and coating the back of the spoon.

Remove from the heat at once and set aside to cool. Serve warm.

COOK'S NOTES
- The chocolate sauces will each set firm once they have cooled, but can be reheated gently to make them runny again.
- When making the Toffee Sauce, take care that the hot sugary mixture doesn't splash you as it bubbles in the pan.
- Do not place the custard over a high heat when cooking as it can easily curdle.

PREPARE AHEAD
The custard can be made up to a day ahead and reheated to serve. All the other sauces can be made ahead and kept in the fridge for up to 2 days.

FREEZE
Apart from the custard, all the sauces freeze well. Bear in mind that if you use frozen raspberries to make the coulis, you won't be able to freeze it again afterwards.

Baking

Ginger Oat Crunch Biscuits

Simple to make, crunchy and very tasty. The mixture does spread out to give very thin, crisp biscuits, so the balls need to be well spaced apart on the baking sheets.

MAKES 36 · PREP TIME: *15 minutes* · COOK TIME: *17 minutes, plus cooling*

150g (5oz) butter, diced if cold (see note)
1 tbsp golden syrup (see note)
175g (6oz) granulated sugar
75g (3oz) self-raising flour
50g (2oz) semolina
100g (4oz) porridge oats (standard or jumbo)
2 tsp ground ginger

Preheat the oven to 180°C/160°C Fan/Gas 4, then line 3–4 baking sheets with baking paper (see note) or line two sheets and cook in batches.

Measure the butter, golden syrup and sugar into a saucepan and warm through over a medium heat until runny.

Remove from the heat and add the flour, semolina, oats and ginger. Stir until well incorporated, then tip on to a baking sheet, flatten out and leave to cool for 10 minutes.

Scoop up teaspoonfuls of the mixture (which will be quite crumbly and buttery) and roll into 36 little balls, then place on the prepared baking sheets, well spaced apart. Push down slightly to flatten and then bake in the oven for about 15 minutes until lightly golden.

Leave to cool on the baking sheets, then store in an airtight container when completely cold.

COOK'S NOTES
· The butter can be used straight from the fridge or at room temperature – it does not matter as it's being melted.
· Coat your spoon in a little oil before measuring the syrup – it will slip off easily and give a more accurate measurement.
· Silicone baking mats are a great alternative to baking paper – the biscuits slide off easily and the mats can be washed and used again.

PREPARE AHEAD
These can be made ahead and stored in an airtight container for up to 3 days.

FREEZE
Freeze the cooked biscuits for up to 3 months. The uncooked dough balls also freeze well.

Light Carrot and Cinnamon Cupcakes

With all the flavour of a traditional full-sized carrot cake, these cupcakes are much quicker to bake and have a delicious cinnamon icing.

MAKES 12 · PREP TIME: *30 minutes* · COOK TIME: *20–25 minutes*

FOR THE SPONGE
2 large eggs
75ml (3fl oz) sunflower oil
150g (5oz) caster sugar
150g (5oz) self-raising flour
1 tsp ground cinnamon
½ tsp bicarbonate of soda
200g (7oz) carrots, peeled and
    finely grated (see note)

FOR THE ICING
75g (3oz) butter, softened
75g (3oz) full-fat cream cheese
350g (12oz) icing sugar, sifted
¼ tsp ground cinnamon

You will need a 12-hole muffin tin and a piping bag with a plain nozzle. Preheat the oven to 180°C/160°C Fan/Gas 4 and line the tin with muffin cases.

Crack the eggs into a large bowl and beat with an electric hand whisk on full speed until the eggs have tripled in volume and the whisk leaves a ribbon-like trail in the mixture when it is lifted out. Add the sunflower oil and whisk again for a few seconds until incorporated. Fold in the dry ingredients, followed by the carrots.

Divide the mixture between the muffin cases and bake in the oven for 20–25 minutes until well risen and just springing back to the touch.

Remove from the oven and leave to cool on a wire rack.

Meanwhile, whisk the butter and cream cheese until smooth using the electric whisk. Add half of the icing sugar and beat again. Add the remaining icing sugar and the cinnamon and beat until light and fluffy. Spoon into the piping bag and pipe a swirl of icing on top of each bun to serve (see note).

COOK'S NOTES
· It would be quicker to use a coarse grater if you don't mind having flecks of carrot in the buns.
· If time is short, just dollop the icing on top with a teaspoon.

PREPARE AHEAD
Bake and ice the cupcakes up to 6 hours ahead. Once iced, they will keep for a day or so, but because of the cream cheese in the icing it's best to store them in the fridge and then serve at room temperature.

FREEZE
These freeze well for up to a month, ideally without the icing.

Blueberry American Muffins

These are like the traditional American muffins so don't expect them to be very sweet. They are always best served warm.

MAKES 12 · PREP TIME: *10 minutes* · COOK TIME: *20–25 minutes*

275g (10oz) self-raising flour
1 tsp baking powder
2 eggs
75g (3oz) caster sugar
225ml (8fl oz) milk
100g (4oz) butter, melted and
    cooled slightly
1 tsp vanilla extract (see note)
175g (6oz) fresh blueberries

You will need a 12-hole muffin tin. Preheat the oven to 200°c/180°c Fan/Gas 6 and line the muffin tin with paper cases.

Measure all the ingredients except the blueberries into a bowl and mix with a wooden spoon until just combined. Take care not to overwork the mixture. Stir in the blueberries, then divide evenly between the paper cases.

Bake in the middle of the oven for 20–25 minutes or until risen, cooked through and lightly golden.

Remove to a wire rack to cool slightly before serving.

COOK'S NOTE
Always use vanilla extract as this is a natural flavouring made from the pod; vanilla essence is an artificial flavouring.

PREPARE AHEAD
Best made on the day of serving.

FREEZE
Freeze on the same day and keep in the freezer for about 1 month.

Apricot Buns with Lemon Icing

Children will enjoy these and have fun icing them. They aren't fancy – just a lovely light sponge, made with a little dried apricot, and drizzled with a glacé lemon icing.

MAKES 12 BUNS · PREP TIME: *10 minutes* · **COOK TIME:** *15–18 minutes, plus cooling*

FOR THE SPONGE
100g (4oz) caster sugar
100g (4oz) baking spread, straight from the fridge
100g (4oz) self-raising flour
1 tsp baking powder
2 eggs
50g (2oz) ready-to-eat dried apricots, roughly chopped (see note)

FOR THE ICING
75g (3oz) icing sugar, sifted
½ tbsp fresh lemon juice

You will need a 12-hole bun tin.

Preheat the oven to 180°C/160°C Fan/Gas 4 and line the tin with fairy cake cases.

Measure the sugar, baking spread, flour and baking powder into a large bowl, add the eggs and chopped apricots and whisk with an electric hand whisk until smooth (see note).

Divide evenly between the paper cases – allowing around 1 heaped tablespoon per cake – and bake for about 15–18 minutes, until well risen and lightly golden.

Leave to cool on a wire rack until cold.

Meanwhile, mix the icing sugar and lemon juice together in a bowl until smooth. Once the buns are cold, using a teaspoon, drizzle the icing over the buns in a random pattern.

COOK'S NOTES
· You may find it quicker to snip the apricot into pieces using scissors.
· Be careful not to overbeat the mixture as that would give a dense rather than a light sponge.

PREPARE AHEAD
The buns can be made and iced 1–2 days ahead. Store in an airtight container.

FREEZE
The buns freeze well for up to a month.

Orange, Lemon and Lime Cupcakes

Citrus cupcakes with a gentle, sharp flavour. For a more citrusy flavour
to the frosting, swap the milk for the juice of the orange, lemon or lime.

MAKES 12 · PREP TIME: *15 minutes* · COOK TIME: *20–25 minutes, plus cooling*

FOR THE SPONGE
125g (4½oz) baking spread
175g (6oz) self-raising flour
175g (6oz) caster sugar
3 large eggs
finely grated zest of ½ orange,
   ½ lemon and ½ lime

FOR THE FROSTING
125g (4½oz) butter, softened
250g (9oz) icing sugar, sifted
1–2 tbsp milk (or fruit juice)
finely grated zest of ½ orange,
   ½ lemon and ½ lime

You will need a 12-hole bun tin and a piping bag fitted with a small star nozzle. Preheat the oven to 180°c / 160°c Fan / Gas 4 and line the tin with cupcake cases.

Place all the ingredients for the sponge in a large bowl and beat with an electric hand whisk until light and fluffy (see note). Divide the mixture between the paper cases and bake in the oven for about 20–25 minutes until well risen and lightly golden.

Remove from the oven and leave to cool on a wire rack.

To make the frosting, measure the butter, sugar and 1 tablespoon of the milk into a large bowl. Beat using an electric hand whisk until the mixture is pale and fluffy, adding the remaining milk to loosen if necessary. Mix in the citrus zest, then spoon the frosting into the piping bag and pipe little stars on top of the cakes to serve.

COOK'S NOTE
Be careful not to over-mix the sponge or the frosting, as the sponge will be dense and the frosting difficult to pipe.

PREPARE AHEAD
The cupcakes can be made and frosted up to 6 hours ahead.

FREEZE
Freeze the cupcakes without the frosting, which will freeze well in a separate tub, or even a plastic icing bag, ready to defrost and pipe as needed.

Fast Cheesy Herb Muffins

Savoury muffins are so much quicker to make than bread. The texture is different, of course, but they are superb with soup, salads or for eating on the go. The cheese is lovely and oozy if you serve them warm. Eaten cold, they are still fragrant, with a nice saltiness from the cheese and olives. As with all muffins, this is a slightly moist and heavier bake, rather than a light and airy sponge.

MAKES 12 · PREP TIME: *15 minutes* · COOK TIME: *18–20 minutes*

275g (10oz) self-raising flour
1 tsp baking powder
½ tsp salt
50g (2oz) butter, melted
1 large egg, beaten
250ml (9fl oz) milk
75g (3oz) Gruyère, grated
leaves of 1 bunch of basil,
   chopped
75g (3oz) pitted black olives,
   chopped
2 tbsp sun-dried tomato paste

You will need a 12-hole muffin tin. Preheat the oven to 200°C/ 180°C Fan/Gas 6 and line the tin with muffin cases (see note).

Measure the flour, baking powder and salt into a large bowl. Mix the butter, egg and milk together in a jug.

Add the cheese, basil and olives to the bowl of dry ingredients and mix well. Pour in the wet ingredients and gently stir everything together using a fork. Mix in the sun-dried tomato paste right at the end to give a rippled effect through the batter (see note).

Divide the mixture between the cases and bake in the oven for 18–20 minutes, until well risen and lightly golden brown.

Remove from the oven and allow to cool slightly.

Serve warm or cold.

COOK'S NOTES
- If you can't find muffin cases, you could use cupcake cases; they are larger than fairy cake cases, but not quite as deep as muffin cases, so the mixture may stretch to a few extra muffins.
- Gently swirl in the sun-dried tomato paste, without stirring it in completely, as this gives a lovely hit of tomato when you eat the muffin, as well as a nice rippled effect.

PREPARE AHEAD
Best made and eaten on the day but will keep for 2 days in the fridge in an airtight container.

FREEZE
The muffins freeze well for up to a month. Defrost and warm through at a low heat in the oven to refresh.

Figgy Oat Squares

These are chewy, oaty and very moreish. The figs are semi-dried, so they are a bit squidgy – like ready-to-eat apricots. You could swap the sunflower seeds for pumpkin seeds or even flaked almonds, if you like.

MAKES 16 • PREP TIME: *10 minutes* • COOK TIME: *20–25 minutes, plus cooling*

150g (5oz) butter
75g (3oz) golden syrup
75g (3oz) light muscovado sugar
175g (6oz) porridge oats
50g (2oz) soft dried figs, finely chopped
15g (½oz) sunflower seeds

You will need an 18cm (7in) shallow square cake tin. Preheat the oven to 180°C/160°C Fan/Gas 4 and line the base of the tin with baking paper.

Measure the butter, golden syrup and sugar into a large saucepan and place over a gentle heat. Heat through until the butter has melted and the sugar has dissolved and is smooth. Remove from the heat and stir in the oats, figs and sunflower seeds.

Spoon into the prepared tin, level the surface and bake in the oven for 20–25 minutes, until evenly golden and just firm to touch (see note).

Leave to cool in the tin for about 10 minutes, then score with a knife into 16 squares. Loosen any edges that have stuck to the tin, then leave to become completely cold before turning out and slicing into squares.

COOK'S NOTE
Don't expect these squares to be crisp like flapjacks – they are soft and delicious!

PREPARE AHEAD
Keep for up to 4 days in an airtight container.

FREEZE
These freeze well for up to a month.

Cherry, Almond and Chocolate 10-Minute Squares

Also known as fridge biscuits, these make a lovely sweet treat. They are cut up into small squares as they are quite rich – just a mouthful is plenty. Swap the almonds for another type of chopped nut, if you prefer.

MAKES 25 • PREP TIME: *10 minutes* • CHILL TIME: *1 hour*

FOR THE BASE
75g (3oz) digestive biscuits
40g (1½oz) butter

FOR THE TOPPING
50g (2oz) butter
50ml (2fl oz) milk
30g (1oz) cocoa powder, sifted
300g (11oz) icing sugar, sifted
50g (2oz) dark chocolate,
    broken into pieces
50g (2oz) blanched almonds,
    roughly chopped
50g (2oz) glacé cherries,
    chopped

You will need a 15cm (6in) square cake tin. Grease the tin and line with baking paper.

First make the biscuit base. Crumble the biscuits using a rolling pin to crush into fine crumbs. Melt the butter in a small saucepan, then stir in the crushed biscuits and mix until combined. Spoon into the prepared tin and press down using the back of a spoon until level. Put in the fridge to chill and firm up while you are making the topping.

Melt the butter in a medium saucepan over a medium heat. Add the milk, stir in the cocoa powder and icing sugar and stir until well combined and the mixture is smooth. Remove from the heat, add the chocolate and stir until melted, then mix in the almonds and cherries (see note). The mixture will start to thicken as it cools. Spoon into the tin and spread out to cover the biscuit base.

Chill in the fridge for 1 hour before slicing into 25 squares.

COOK'S NOTE
It's important to add the chocolate to the hot sugar mixture so it melts immediately. It's lovely and glossy at this stage, so add the nuts and cherries, and smooth it over the biscuit base before it cools too much.

PREPARE AHEAD
Prepare the squares up to a day ahead. Once made, store in the fridge.

FREEZE
These freeze well.

Scone Fruit Crown

Making mini scones and gathering them together in a crown shape is a quick and impressive way to serve large numbers for a picnic or other gathering.

MAKES 1 × 18-SCONE CROWN · PREP TIME: *10 minutes* · COOK TIME: *10–12 minutes*

1 egg
about 110ml (3½fl oz) milk
225g (8oz) self-raising flour,
    plus extra for dusting
1 heaped tsp baking powder
40g (1½oz) butter, softened,
    plus extra for greasing
25g (1oz) caster sugar
25g (1oz) sultanas
25g (1oz) ready-to-eat dried
    apricots, chopped into tiny
    pieces (see note)

TO DECORATE
2 tbsp apricot jam, warmed
1–2 tbsp nibbed sugar

You will need a 23cm (9in) round sandwich tin and a 4cm (1½in) plain round pastry cutter. Preheat the oven to 220°C/200°C Fan/ Gas 7 and grease the tin.

Break the egg into a measuring jug, then beat with a fork and pour in enough of the milk to make 150ml (5fl oz) of liquid.

Measure the flour, baking powder and butter into a large bowl. Rub the butter into the flour with your fingertips until it resembles fine breadcrumbs. Add the sugar and, using a fork, stir in enough of the beaten egg to make a sticky dough (reserve any leftover for brushing). Finally, stir in the dried fruits.

Tip on to a floured work surface and gently knead until combined. Don't overwork the mixture or the finished scones will be tough. Using a rolling pin, gently roll out the dough to about 2.5cm (1in) thick. Cut out 18 mini scones with the pastry cutter, re-rolling the dough as needed (see note), and arrange them in the tin so they are touching each other in a crown shape. Brush the tops with the remaining egg mixture from the jug.

Bake in the oven for 10–12 minutes until golden.

Brush with a little apricot jam to glaze and sprinkle with nibbed sugar. Transfer to a wire rack to cool a little, then serve with jam and clotted cream.

COOK'S NOTES
· Use scissors to snip the apricots into pieces quickly.
· Dip your cutter in flour if you find it is getting sticky. (Try not to twist the cutter or the scones will rise unevenly.) Shape any extra dough into another scone and cook alongside the crown – cook's perks!

PREPARE AHEAD
The scone crown is best made and eaten on the same day – served warm, ideally – but it can be made a day ahead. Store in an airtight container.

FREEZE
Freezes well for up to a month.

Apple and Lemon Sandwich Cake

The ultimate cream sponge cake – the apple makes the cake really moist and the lemon-flavoured cream keeps it fresh-tasting. Delicious!

SERVES 6–8 • PREP TIME: *20 minutes* • COOK TIME: *25–30 minutes, plus cooling*

FOR THE SPONGE
225g (8oz) baking spread, straight from the fridge, plus extra for greasing
225g (8oz) caster sugar
225g (8oz) self-raising flour
1 tsp baking powder
4 large eggs, beaten
2 eating apples, peeled, cored and grated (see note)
icing sugar, for dusting

FOR THE LEMON FILLING
150ml (5fl oz) double cream
3 tbsp lemon curd

You will need two 20cm (8in) round, loose-bottomed sandwich tins. Preheat the oven to 180°c/160°c Fan/Gas 4, then grease each tin and line the base with a disc of baking paper.

Measure all the sponge ingredients except the apple and icing sugar into a large bowl and beat with an electric hand whisk until combined. Fold the grated apple into the mixture, then divide between the tins and level the tops.

Bake in the oven for about 25–30 minutes until golden, well risen and coming away from the sides of the tins. Allow to cool in the tins.

Meanwhile, make the filling. Whip the cream into soft peaks, then lightly swirl in the lemon curd. Invert the tins to remove the cakes and then peel away the paper. Sit one cake upside down on a serving plate. Spread the lemon cream to the edge of the sponge, place the other cake gently on top to sandwich the cakes together.

Dust the top with icing sugar to serve.

COOK'S NOTE
For a speedy way to grate the apple, first core the apple and cut into pieces but keep the skin on. Grate the flesh and then discard the skin.

PREPARE AHEAD
Once assembled, keep the cake in the fridge for up to 1 day but serve at room temperature.

FREEZE
The cooked sponges freeze well.

Chocolate Chip Traybake
with Vanilla Mascarpone Icing

A traybake is such a simple, easy type of cake to make, and very quick to mix using the all-in-one method.

MAKES 16 PIECES · PREP TIME: *15 minutes* · COOK TIME: *35 minutes, plus cooling*

FOR THE SPONGE
4 tbsp cocoa powder, sifted
4 tbsp boiling water
4 large eggs
225g (8oz) baking spread,
    straight from the fridge,
    plus extra for greasing
225g (8oz) caster sugar
225g (8oz) self-raising flour
1 tsp baking powder
100g (4oz) dark chocolate
    chips

FOR THE ICING
250g (9oz) full-fat mascarpone
    cheese
3 tbsp icing sugar, sifted
1 tsp vanilla extract
cocoa powder, for dusting

You will need a 23 × 30cm (9 × 12in) traybake tin. Preheat the oven to 180°C/160°C Fan/Gas 4 and grease and line the tin with baking paper.

First make the sponge. Measure the cocoa powder and boiling water into a large bowl and mix with a spoon into a smooth paste. Add all the remaining sponge ingredients except the chocolate chips and mix together using an electric hand whisk until light and fluffy in texture (see note). Stir in the chocolate chips.

Spoon the sponge mixture into the prepared tin and level the surface. Bake in the middle of the oven for about 35 minutes, until the cake is coming away from the sides of the tin and is springy to the touch in the middle.

Leave to cool in the tin on a wire rack.

To make the icing, mix the mascarpone, icing sugar and vanilla extract together in a bowl. Spread over the surface of the cold cake and dust with cocoa powder to finish.

Slice into about 16 pieces – squares or fingers – to serve.

COOK'S NOTE
Whisk the sponge for no more than 4 minutes as over-mixing can produce a dense cake.

PREPARE AHEAD
Can be made and iced up to 8 hours ahead.

FREEZE
Freezes well, without the icing, for up to a month.

White Chocolate and Hazelnut Traybake

Chocolate and nuts have always gone well together and they combine beautifully here – the hazelnuts giving a lovely crunch that offsets the creamy texture of the cake. The recipe also works well with chopped almonds instead of hazelnuts.

MAKES 24 PIECES · PREP TIME: *15 minutes* · COOK TIME: *30–35 minutes, plus cooling*

FOR THE SPONGE
250g (9oz) baking spread, plus
    extra for greasing
250g (9oz) caster sugar
1 tsp baking powder
4 large eggs
3 tbsp milk
1 tsp vanilla extract
250g (9oz) self-raising flour
100g (4oz) white chocolate,
    chopped into chunks
    (see note)
25g (1oz) chopped roasted
    hazelnuts (see note)

FOR THE FROSTING
75g (3oz) white chocolate
100g (4oz) butter, softened
150g (5oz) icing sugar, sifted
25g (1oz) chopped roasted
    hazelnuts

You will need a 23 × 30cm (9 × 12in) traybake tin. Preheat the oven to 180°c/160°c Fan/Gas 4, then grease the tin and line with baking paper.

Measure the baking spread, caster sugar and baking powder into a large bowl and add the eggs, milk, vanilla extract and flour. Beat with an electric hand whisk until light and fluffy, then stir in the chocolate and hazelnuts.

Spoon into the tin and level the surface. Bake in the oven for about 30–35 minutes until well risen and lightly golden.

Leave to cool in the tin on a wire rack and then remove from the tin.

To make the frosting while the cake is cooling, first melt the chocolate in a bowl set over a pan of gently simmering water. Whisk the butter and sugar together with the electric whisk until light and fluffy, then stir in the melted chocolate. Spread over the cooled cake and sprinkle with the hazelnuts.

Cut into 24 pieces to serve.

COOK'S NOTES
· For speed, use white chocolate chips instead.
· Buy the hazelnuts already chopped and pre-roasted (for both the sponge and the frosting) to save time.

PREPARE AHEAD
Make up to 8 hours ahead.

FREEZE
Freezes well, without the icing, for up to a month.

Quick Icings

These would all be perfect for a sandwich cake or for topping about 12 individual cupcakes.

Coffee Buttercream Icing

MAKES 325G (11½OZ) · PREP TIME: *10 minutes, plus cooling*

2 tsp instant coffee granules
2 tsp boiling water from
    the kettle
100g (4oz) butter, softened
225g (8oz) icing sugar, sifted

Measure the coffee granules into a bowl, add the boiling water and stir until smooth, then allow to cool. Add the butter and sugar to the bowl and beat with an electric hand whisk until pale and fluffy.

White Chocolate Icing

MAKES 400G (14OZ) · PREP TIME: *5 minutes* · COOK TIME: *5 minutes, plus cooling*

100g (4oz) good-quality white
    chocolate (ideally Belgian
    or Swiss)
50g (2oz) butter, softened
75g (3oz) full-fat cream cheese
200g (7oz) icing sugar, sifted
½ tsp vanilla extract

Melt the white chocolate in a bowl set over a pan of just simmering water and stir until runny. Set aside to cool and thicken a little. Meanwhile, whisk together the butter, cream cheese, icing sugar and vanilla extract until soft and fluffy. Stir in the cooled melted chocolate.

Lemon Mascarpone Icing

MAKES 400G (14OZ) · PREP TIME: *10 minutes, plus optional chilling*

250g (9oz) full-fat mascarpone
    cheese
150g (5oz) good-quality lemon
    curd
juice of ½ lemon

Spoon the mascarpone into a bowl and beat until smooth. Stir in the lemon curd and gradually add the lemon juice – just enough to ensure that the mixture is smooth and fluffy, but not too runny. Chill in the fridge, if necessary, to allow it to thicken up.

Chocolate Ganache Icing

MAKES 300G (11OZ) · PREP TIME: *5 minutes* · COOK TIME: *5 minutes, plus cooling*

150g (5oz) dark chocolate
  (less than 70% cocoa
  solids), broken into pieces
150ml (5fl oz) double cream

Place the chocolate and cream in a bowl set over a pan of just simmering water and allow to melt together until smooth and runny. Stir the mixture, then remove from the heat and leave to cool and thicken up.

Chocolate Fudge Icing

MAKES 325G (11½OZ) · PREP TIME: *5 minutes* · COOK TIME: *5 minutes, plus cooling*

50g (2oz) butter
25g (1oz) cocoa powder, sifted
3 tbsp milk
225g (8oz) icing sugar, sifted

Melt the butter in a saucepan over a medium heat. Add the cocoa powder and stir over a high heat, allowing the mixture to bubble for 1 minute. Add the milk and icing sugar and stir to combine. Remove from the heat and set aside to cool and thicken.

COOK'S NOTE
Cover the surface of each of the icings with cling film until ready to use – this will stop them drying out.

PREPARE AHEAD
The Coffee Buttercream Icing, Chocolate Ganache Icing and Chocolate Fudge Icing will all keep, covered, for 3–4 days. The White Chocolate Icing and the Lemon Mascarpone Icing are best used on the day they are made.

Quick Meal Ideas

Midweek meals in 20 minutes

- Spinach, Cabbage and Mushroom Stir-Fry
- Tagliatelle with Mushrooms and Stilton
- King Prawn and Broccoli Stir-Fry with Black Bean Sauce
- Spaghetti alle Vongole
- Ginger Teriyaki Salmon
- Marinated Mango Pork Medallions
- Piquant Chicken with Tomato and Peppers

Meals to make ahead

- Spiced Chicken Lettuce Cups
- Midweek Chicken, Mozzarella and Tomato Bake
- Speedy Thai Chicken and Vegetable Curry
- Chicken and Mushroom Suet Crust Pie
- Quick Beef Ragú
- Thai Green Beef Curry
- Cauliflower and Potato Cakes
- Upside-Down Rhubarb Pudding with Caramel Sauce
- Rum and Raisin Ice Cream

Fast vegetarian meals

- Asparagus, Feta, Pea and Olive Salad
- Squash, Goat's Cheese and Quinoa Salad
- Rice Noodle and Vegetable Stir-Fry
- Cauliflower, Aubergine and Lemon Grass Thai Curry
- Vegetable Kebabs
- Nutty Wholemeal Couscous Salad
- Pan-Fried Halloumi with Quick, Fresh Tomato Chutney

Quick to prepare, slower to cook

- All-in-one Sausage and Egg Breakfast
- Burgundy Chicken
- Dry-Roasted Chicken Tikka
- Korma-Style Chicken Curry
- Chicken and Asparagus Fricassée
- Lamb Tagine
- Quick Beef Ragú
- Spiced Roasted Squash
- Pear, Ginger and Almond Brioche Tart
- Rum and Raisin Ice Cream

20-minute desserts

- Gooseberry and Elderflower Fool
- Chocolate Cappuccino Tart
- Piccoli Tiramisù
- Glazed Pineapple with Rum and Lime
- Passion Fruit and Orange Cheesecake
- Limoncello Trifle

Easy weekend feasts

- Pan-Fried Scallops with Leeks and Tarragon
- Beef Fillet with Creamy Stilton and Mushroom Sauce
- Sea Bass en Papillote with Courgette Ribbons
- Roast Venison with Peppercorn Sauce
- Rack of Lamb with Bulgur Wheat and Spiced Yoghurt Sauce
- Crayfish and Prawn Nasi Goreng
- Mushroom and Asparagus Risotto
- White Chocolate and Hazelnut Traybake

When You Have a Little More Time

Making your own stock

Good-quality stock can make all the difference to a recipe, especially when you are cooking something like soup. There are good fresh stocks available in the supermarket but if you have the time it's worth making your own. If you do, be sure to make enough to freeze some and you'll have home-made stock ready for when time is short. It is useful to freeze the stock in portions – try 150ml (¼ pint), 300ml (½ pint) or 600ml (1 pint) containers.

To make 2.5 litres (4 pints) of chicken stock, place 1.5kg (3lb) raw chicken/game/turkey bones in a stockpot with 2 peeled onions and brown over a medium heat. Pour in 4 litres (7 pints) of water and bring to the boil. Add 3 carrots, 3 celery sticks, a bouquet garni (bay leaves and sprigs of thyme and parsley) and some peppercorns and leave to simmer, half covered, for 2½–3 hours. Strain the contents of the pan into a large bowl, then decant into a container for freezing or use straight away – try the Chicken Noodle Soup on page 68.

You can make a dark stock using cooked chicken/game/turkey bones – after a roast, for example – but raw bones should not be mixed with cooked bones.

If your local butcher is kind enough to give you beef bones, it is possible to make your own beef stock. Lay the bones in a roasting tin and brown in a hot oven (220°c/Fan 200°c/Gas 7). Tip into a stockpot and continue as for chicken stock. Pork and lamb stocks are not worth while making, as they are too fatty.

Vegetables prepared ahead

There are great pre-cooked vegetables available in supermarkets (and I use a number of them in the recipes in this book) but if you have time to spare, here are two veg that are even nicer prepared yourself. They can be made ahead and kept in the fridge for when you need them.

BEETROOT
Select beetroot of about the same size so they cook at the same rate. Trim the leaves to about 10cm (4in) – if trimmed right down the colour will bleed out as it cooks and the beetroot will lose its flavour. Place the beetroot in a pan and cover with water. Bring to the boil, then reduce the heat and simmer for about 1 hour, or until tender. Leave to cool, then peel. The cooked beetroot will keep for 4 days in the fridge.

ROAST PEPPERS
The roasted peppers you can buy in a jar are a delicious and easy addition to a recipe, especially the peppers in oil, but if you have time and raw peppers in the fridge then you can roast your own very simply. Preheat the grill and line the grill pan with foil. Cut the peppers in half, remove the seeds and arrange the peppers cut side down in the grill pan. Grill, turning regularly, until blackened all over. Remove the peppers to a bowl, cover with a plate and leave to cool – the steam will loosen the skin. Strip off and discard all the black skin, then cut each pepper into strips. You can use these roasted pepper strips in any number of recipes – try the Romano Pepper and Herb Penne on page 174 – or store them in sterilised jars for another day (see overleaf).

Making your own lemon curd

Lemon curd is actually very easy to make and, while shop-bought varieties are good for when you are in a hurry (be sure to buy luxury curd made with pure ingredients), it's lovely to make your own. Break 4 eggs into a saucepan and whisk to combine. Stir in 300g (10½oz) sugar, 225g (8oz) butter, cut into pieces, and the finely grated zest and juice of 4 lemons. Once everything is combined, place the pan over a medium heat and whisk continuously until the mixture coats the back of a spoon and is slightly thickened – this could take 7–10 minutes. Do not allow the mixture to boil or it may split. If you are an inexperienced cook, whisk the curd in a bowl over simmering water. It will take longer but is foolproof. Remove from the heat and leave to cool before serving.

Sterilising jars

If you are making pesto (see page 190) or home-made curd (see left), it is a good idea to make more than you need so you can store it in sterilised jars for when time is short. Preheat the oven to 120°C/Fan 100°C and wash the jars thoroughly. Place the jars in the oven, with space between them, for 10–15 minutes. You could also place them in a pan of boiling water for 10 minutes, then drain upside down on a clean tea towel. Quickest of all, though, would be to put them through a hot wash in the dishwasher!

Index

Thank Yous

Quick Cooking was quite a challenge to write and it was such a bonus to have the usual wonderful team to create and test the recipes.

After 29 years working together, Lucy Young is my closest friend – together we decided on the concept 'Quick', which totally fits in with our lives these days. Luce is a perfectionist but is also decidedly practical and is completely dedicated to every detail. Lucinda McCord works with us one day a week and, once again, has excelled with the recipe testing. She is a treasure, we could not do without her.

Lisa Harrison and Evie Harbury recreated the recipes for the photographs in the book and, along with Isla Murray, as home economists for the TV series, all took so much care, precision and devotion to the food being perfect. Photographer Georgia Glynn Smith did her magic with the click of the camera – the photo shoots are always great fun and no one can wait to finish a shot so they can enjoy the dishes.

Lizzy Gray, the publisher, always listened to our requests and made sure the book reflected our idea. Jo Roberts-Miller has edited the book with her undoubted skill – no one could have been more involved and her expertise is second to none. Thanks also to Clare Skeats the designer, Polly Webb Wilson the props stylist, and to Jan Stevens, Anne Harnan and Vicky Pettipher for additional recipe testing.

To the TV crew at Sidney St for the fun *Quick* series filming and the fabulous crew led by Karen Ross, Dave Crearer and Alice Binks. You are a joy to work with. To my literary agent Felicity Bryan and media agent Joanna Kaye at KBJ – thanks to their teams for holding our hands.

We push the boat out for each book and this is no exception, thanks to the fabulous team.

Love Mary

1 3 5 7 9 10 8 6 4 2

BBC Books, an imprint of Ebury Publishing
20 Vauxhall Bridge Road,
London SW1V 2SA

BBC Books is part of the Penguin Random House group of companies whose addresses can be found at global.penguinrandomhouse.com

 Penguin
Random House
UK

Photography by Georgia Glynn-Smith

Mary Berry has asserted her right to be identified as the author of this Work in accordance with the Copyright, Designs and Patents Act 1988

First published by BBC Books in 2019

www.penguin.co.uk

A CIP catalogue record for this book is available from the British Library

ISBN 9781785943898

Publishing Director: Lizzy Gray
Project Editor: Jo Roberts-Miller
Food Stylist: Lisa Harrison
Food Stylist Assistant: Evie Harbury
Prop Stylist: Polly Webb Wilson
Cover Designer: Two Associates
Text Designer: Clare Skeats
Testing: Jan Stevens, Anne Harnan and Vicky Pettipher
Copyeditor: Kate Parker
Production: Helen Everson

Colour reproduction by Alta Image, London

Printed and bound in Germany by Mohn Media GmbH

Penguin Random House is committed to a sustainable future for our business, our readers and our planet. This book is made from Forest Stewardship Council® certified paper.

MIX
Paper from responsible sources
FSC® C018179